emma and her selves

emma and her selves:

a memoir of treatment and a therapist's self-discovery

may benatar

for eda, of blessed memory

epigraph

In the creation myth of mystical Judaism, the world begins with a shattering. The Infinite, in Hebrew *Ein Sof*, contracted in order to make room for our Universe, for creation. From that contraction came darkness. When *Ein Sof* declared, "let there be light," ten holy vessels were created to carry the primordial light to our world. The vessels, unable to contain the perfection of Ein Sof, cracked and the light broke into pieces that scattered throughout the world.

Each human soul, it is said, possesses a sliver, a shard of the light of creation. There is light buried even in the darkest of souls. The purpose of human life is to raise these sparks to the heavens, to unite with other sparks, thus healing the divine Cosmos. Healing is the purpose of life. Uniting the sparks is its goal. The work of our souls is integration.

Rabbi Isaac Luria—the 16th-century Kabbalist and originator of this creation myth—and other Spanish Jews were living in exile in Safed, a town in what is now known as Israel. They had been persecuted and expelled from Spain and Portugal, their communities destroyed. The trauma of the Inquisition was fresh. Luria imagined creation in the form of a shattering and a formula for repair, pointing a way towards survival and reconstitution. The metaphor works perfectly both for the effects of individual and communal trauma and their healing.

As a psychotherapist as well as on a personal level as a Jew of the Diaspora, a spark separated from other sparks, I find this creation myth of mystical Judaism deeply appealing. Sometimes my work as a clinician has been to address and literally converse with the splintered parts of an individual's personality and to guide them toward wholeness, towards integration.

Emma, the young woman whose treatment I unwittingly undertook in 1990 and whose (imperfect) healing took me through almost two decades of my own professional and personal development, needed to unite the shards of her own shattering, the consequence of extreme trauma in and throughout her childhood. That was my work with Emma.

contents

how I became a trauma therapist

In the 1980s, I began to work with individuals identified by themselves or by therapists as survivors of childhood sexual abuse. My introduction to this work was somewhat serendipitous, but over time it became the work that absorbed me the most and energized my psychotherapy practice. I studied, trained and applied myself to becoming an effective and informed clinician for this special population of individuals with chronic, complex post-traumatic stress disorder. Fewer than 10 years into this work, I met Emma, a woman I came to understand as suffering from Multiple Personality Disorder. I knew her for over two decades and treated her actively for 15 of those years. Knowing her, treating her, wrestling with her much as Jacob wrestled with the Angel, transformed my understanding of trauma and its profound effects; it informed my treatment of all patients; and finally it deepened my understanding of myself. This is where my journey began.

For two years—several years before I met Emma—I worked with a nearly mute woman. Frances held herself tightly, rigid with fright. She was young, in her mid-20s, tall, thin and very sad. I knew she had a history of sexual abuse but I did not know who had abused her, the nature of the abuse, or details of the family she came from. With only the vaguest notion of what the issues were for her or why she wouldn't speak, I didn't know what she needed. In an effort to connect I just talked to her, trying to guess what she was feeling and reflecting it back to her.

Frances was not like any of the other clients I had been treating at the counseling center. She seemed unable to engage. Many years later, she told me, "A little girl was there from the beginning, hiding behind your chair while we were in session." Her terror and trauma were personified by this mute child. I didn't know it then, but after a long, *long* time, I came to understand that Frances was my first highly dissociated client.

Frances came to me in the early 1980s after a colleague and I had attended an inspiring conference at Harvard University on the psychology of women. One paper on sexual violence against women stood out among the many wonderful talks. There was nothing dramatic about the presenter's style; she was pretty low key. But the material was dramatic, her talk was riveting.

Judith Lewis Herman a young psychiatrist not much older than I, asked of the 900 mostly female psychotherapists in attendance, "How many of you have been mugged?" People raised their hands. She went on to say that she could not ask for a show of hands of victims of sexual violence, as victims of these crimes are stigmatized. "Secrecy is rooted in shaming the victim and discrediting her story," she said. The victim is the one left with the shame, silenced and damaged by it. The perpetrator is mostly unknown and unmarked.

Judith Herman's paper turned out to be life changing for me; it was a key moment in shaping my identity as a psychotherapist. My colleague and I stood together during the break sipping tea, munching croissants and sharing bits and pieces of our life story, intimate pieces. We were moved by both the paper and by Herman's tribute to her recently deceased mother, who had been scheduled to deliver a paper at this conference as well. Herman saw mothers as the natural protectors of their female children and the strength of the mother-daughter bond as the best bulwark against sexual violence. At the break, dozens of women flocked to the pay phones to call their mothers. Women and mothers had been honored that day, the wounds of women witnessed in an open and welcoming way.

Both the women's movement and the anti-war movement of the '70s had fueled interest in and investigation of the twin issues of trauma effects and violence against women. Judy Herman inspired me to carry the torch and her impassioned message to the mental health staff with whom I worked, to the town in which I lived, to the people I knew. Eventually I taught this material to graduate students, but it started with my presentation at a staff meeting.

I was a staff member at a counseling center where the therapists were mostly male. The material I presented to them was new and not particularly welcomed by that group. Nonetheless, I brought my experience of the conference and Herman's meticulously researched paper to them, excited about and empowered by what I had learned; so I was taken aback by questions like: "Is this really true, that one in three women have been sexually abused by the age of 18?"

In the early '80s, the notion that large numbers of women and children might be victims of sexual trauma and suffering from its aftereffects had not entered the mainstream. I distinctly remember one male staff member asking, chuckling, "*Could* one actually rape one's wife?" Is it rape if you are married? I was outraged by this comment; it was many years later, 1993, before all 50 states had passed laws criminalizing rape between married men and their wives. However, after that staff presentation, I became known as the resident "expert" on sexual abuse.

Shortly after the presentation, a therapist who was seeing a couple learned in the initial session that the wife, Frances, had a history of sexual abuse. "We have someone who is an expert on sexual abuse," he told Frances, and referred her to me. I knew the truth: no one on that all-male staff wanted to touch this. But I was new at the counseling center and I was game.

Working with Frances turned out to be very challenging. The marriage that had brought her into the treatment failed quickly. We didn't talk much about it, or about her sexual abuse history. We didn't talk about much at all, as she barely spoke to during those two years. When she did speak, her sentences were short and typically unrevealing. The victim's shame that Herman spoke of in her talk seemed to leak from Frances' pores.

Frances cancelled appointments more often than not. I certainly was interested in her and drawn to her sadness, her silent suffering, so I called her each time she cancelled. She always showed up the following week. She asked me, many years later, "Why did you always call me when I cancelled, why did you pursue me?" Truthfully, I have no idea. Whatever the connection was that I felt, it too was voiceless.

I think back on that time and wonder how I managed all that silence. I did strive to know her in some way, even though she was too frightened to tell me who she was. I knew enough not to let the silence stretch on. "It's probably pretty scary to be here," I told her. "Maybe you don't know if this is safe, if this office is safe, if *I* am safe. That's understandable." If I didn't utter these exact words, it was the essence of what I wanted to convey.

Frances' posture and her eyes spoke volumes about her fear, her sense of danger. Her gaze was either downcast or wide-eyed. I think she had no idea what therapy was or how to do it. I didn't know how to engage someone like Frances either, someone so frozen, so terrified, so silenced. My chatter was more about *not* leaving her alone with her fear and dread. The content was less important than that there were words of some sort. I was groping for a thread, a bridge that we could build together. I hoped my facial expression reflected back to her the sadness she manifested and my empathy for that sadness.

Frances never became much of a talker, always dropping in and out of therapy at critical moments in the treatment. But we did construct a bumpy bond over time and most importantly, the little girl, who initially I did not know was there, listened in to what we were doing together and grew up over time. I do have a mental picture of a pale, frightened child huddling, shaking behind my chair during those years, absorbing…something.

Frances started and finished college, the first of her very large family to do so. She became a professional and a mother. She did a pretty good job of raising and providing for her son as a single parent, eventually buying and restoring a house. She survived a severe illness and a near fatal car accident, and rehabilitated herself from both.

In the years to come, I was to treat several even more severely traumatized women who met the criteria for Multiple Personality Disorder (MPD), or Dissociative Identity Disorder (DID) as it later came to be known. Frances and two others remained in treatment for decades. From them, I learned a lot. I suffered a lot. I was changed. The experience in Boston, learning from Judy Herman, the presentation at the staff meeting, my instant designation as "expert," my work with Frances started me on a journey not yet complete.

Why was I so taken with this particular brand of suffering? Maybe it started before that conference. Maybe I was rediscovering an interest that had been unfocused and gotten lost along the way years before. Looking back, many years before going to the conference in Boston, I detect a red thread, a timid but enduring concern for women unrecognized and hurting. I did read *The Feminine Mystique* when it came out in 1963, my first year in college, and bought and sent a copy to my aunt, an educated woman who seemed to me to be mired in domestic detail and drudgery. (She never did read the book; she "didn't have time.") I remember writing a paper in college on pornography as well as one arguing that women in Homer's *Iliad* (or *Odyssey?*) were overlooked by literary critics as major players in the story. These were the '60s before the women's movement made so much noise, so these meagre gestures came from within me, rather than from the ferment of the times. I now know that trauma itself was in my bloodstream. I just didn't know it at the beginning.

Once word got out at the center that I was the resident "expert" on sexual abuse, sexual violence and trauma, I started to work with a number of individuals who identified themselves as having this history. It was only a matter of time before other patients with dissociative disorders, who segregated parts of themselves into discrete, sometimes watertight packages, came my way. Like most therapists of that time, more than 30 years ago, I didn't yet recognize the phenomena of multiple self-states until it screamed in my face. I remember stating authoritatively to a client who was a criminal lawyer and felt that many of her imprisoned clients had "multiple personalities" that "It is highly unlikely, it's a very rare condition." Ha! Clearly I was part of the psychiatric mainstream that dismissed dissociation and its extreme manifestation, multiple identities.

Today we have *Inside Out*, a Pixar movie about animated self- states in the head of a joyous 11-year-old girl. We have the prizewinning memoirist, novelist and essayist Jeanette Winterson, described as deploying characters who "see as mad those who do not embrace the nomadic concept of the fluid multiplicity of selves." (Merja Makinen, from *The Novels of Jeanette Winterson*. Palgrave Macmillan, 2005.) Today we easily grasp the notion that there is the work-self and the self that shows up at home, distinct from that which shows up at parties, sporting events or with intimate friends.

My daughter, like many of us, has three different voice mail messages: work, home, cell phone. At work, the pitch of her voice is low; she is professional, deliberate and someone to be taken seriously. On her cell she is casual, the pitch a little higher. The home voice mail sounds like a different person altogether: peppy, cheerful, the pitch at least an octave above the work voicemail. *That* woman/girl is young, energetic and fun. This is both different and not different from having multiple selves. Each voice mail message conveys the circumstance and the state of being that she occupies in each setting. My daughter has easy access to each "self -state." She remembers what is going on at work when she is at home, and if she has to take a work call at home, amidst preparing dinner and directing the children, she can do so fairly easily and with fluidity.

The difference with Emma, the client who taught me the most about "multiplicity," whose treatment inspired this project, is that she did not have the easy same access to all the self-states that my daughter has. Some "parts" (this is the lingo to describe sequestered ego states in a person with DID) went to work, some parts parented, and many different parts held the trauma memories. Not all of the parts showed up for therapy. Frequently the parts did not know each other, or only some did; communication across the system was poor or non-existent

In DID, parts of experience, the really awful bits, are sequestered in sections of the overall personality so that literally the left hand doesn't know what the right hand knows. *Tommy*, the rock opera written by The Who in the '60s, captures some of what DID is all about.

Tommy—later made into a Broadway musical and a film—is the story of a traumatized little boy who becomes deaf, mute, blind *and* a wizard at pinball, a game where participants generally have keen sight. As a small child, Tommy had all of his senses until he witnessed the murder of his father at the hands of his mother's lover. The lyric tells the rest of the story:

> *What about the boy?*
> *What about the boy?*
> *What about the boy?*
> *He saw it all!*
> (Mother sings to Tommy:)
> *You didn't hear it*
> *You didn't see it.*
> *You won't say nothing to no one*
> *ever in your life.*
> *You never heard it*
> *Oh how absurd it*
> *All seems without any proof.*
> *You didn't hear it*
> *You didn't see it*
> *You never heard it not a word of it.*
> *You won't say nothing to no one*
> *Never tell a soul*
> *What you know is the Truth.*

Little Tommy manages to go blind, deaf, and mute to conform to the pleas and commands of his mother. But he also holds to the truth deep within. It turns out that there is a great way to do this: it's called "dissociation."

We all dissociate to some degree or another. At the extreme end of the DID spectrum, a person bifurcates the mind, holding one reality in one location and another in a deeper, hidden place. The extreme experience of witnessing a murder, or of being sexually abused (also experienced by Tommy), or being on the receiving end of repetitive sadistic violence and torture all create conditions that may manifest as a dissociative disorder.

> *Sickness will surely take the mind*
> *Where minds can't usually go.*
> *Come on the amazing journey*
> *And learn all you should know.*

And I did, I went on that "amazing journey" and it shaped my professional life. It also transformed how I see the human world and myself.

DRAMATIS PERSONAE

Emma: "System Emma" or "the greater Emma" refers to the *entirety* of Emma's internal "ego states." I will refer to these ego states variously as "parts," "sub-personalities," or "self-states." No one term satisfies me as adequately descriptive, so I vary the terms.

Louie: The first of Emma's ego states that appeared in the treatment, initially as a 10-year-old boy, later on as a teen, and eventually as an adult was the same age as Emma. As an adult he was referred to as "Lou."

Louie knew all of the ego states listed below. Much later in the treatment a whole new layer of states emerged that he did not know.

Angel: A spiritual guide who was not considered by "system Emma" to be another ego state, but rather someone outside the system who offered periodic solace and guidance of a spiritual nature. Occasionally I would get guidance from him for the therapy via a letter or a report from Louie. He never made an appearance as did the others, nor did he seem connected to any of the reported trauma.

The Twins

Nan: The twins were both 13 years old when they were created and the same when I met them. Nan, very shy, did not show up much in treatment, but was supportive of the therapy. She was an artist and did provide me with drawings of the various ego states as they appeared to themselves and each other inside.

Eve: The other twin, very resistant to the therapy, sought to undermine the treatment and try to get them out of therapy. Eve was aligned with the abusers. Identifying with perpetrators is perhaps the most common coping mechanism for victims of abuse, and Eve embodied that strategy. At times during Emma's life, Eve was promiscuous, abused drugs and put the greater Emma in peril. She hated me!

Missy: An adult-like, or at least more mature ego state who was created at the time they were all put into foster care. She attended school, interacted with the outside world, often went to work, and was an expert professional. She explained things to me early in the treatment and was a great co-therapist until she integrated and in so doing, strengthened the adult Emma.

Joey/Emmie: Representations of six-year-old children who were best friends. Joey was a real boy, a friend of Emma, who died, hit by a car in her presence. She kept him alive by bringing him inside. Emmie was very shy, but eventually grew into a more Missy-like girl with many strengths. By the end of treatment, she sounded to me a lot like Missy.

Joey reminded me of a young Louie once he came forward; but got darker, more tortured as he remembered more of what had happened to them when they were young. His clairvoyance and connection to spiritual guides was an important feature of his character.

Benji: the terror in my office. Later called Ben, Benji held the worst memories and was the last to do substantial work in therapy.

chapter two
introducing emma, dissociation and did

"Dissociation is the essence of trauma."
—Bessel van der Kolk, 2014

This is a not a case record but a memoir of my treatment of a woman, Emma, diagnosed with Dissociative Identity Disorder (DID), formerly known as Multiple Personality Disorder (MPD). Unlike a case study, it is incomplete and contains very little description of her abuse history, so as to protect both my former client's privacy and the reader, for the details are ghastly. We worked very intensively over a period of 20 years with some interruptions, meeting twice a week for extended sessions. My goal is to share what the experience of psychotherapy was like both for Emma and for me.

The story also tracks my development as a therapist and my growth as a person; both processes key to a successful treatment in so complex and challenging a case. In a way I was required to "grow" my own ego states to meet the exigencies that Emma presented. The therapist can't easily leave "parts" of themselves outside the door if they desire to be effective practitioners.

Emma entered treatment with me in early 1990. A mentor and teacher of hers recognized the post-traumatic nature of Emma's difficulties and referred her to the counseling center where I was on staff. Emma presumably was seeking treatment for depression. With two young children and a busy school and work schedule, there were times she had trouble functioning effectively. She knew that her father, a violent alcoholic, had both physically and sexually abused her, but had great difficulty being coherent about what turned out to be a horrendous history of brutality throughout her childhood. All of this took time to unfold.

Emma was vague but likeable; she showed up regularly and on time for sessions. She wanted to get better, to be a better mom and wife, but at the outset I was not sure what specific effects of her history were troubling her. She was not ready to tell me that she was losing time—blanking out for periods—but that was happening and led to many difficulties.

In order to treat Emma, I had to learn a host of new skills and new concepts that weren't yet widely taught in my field. It is not within my capacity to capture more than a fraction of the process of our work together. I have had to settle for a detailed description of the main characters as I came to know and experience them: some of their motivations, history and what it was like to live and learn with all of them as we toiled together to bring Emma to a safer place in her life. The individual sub-personalities are presented the way I experienced them and as I would like the reader to experience them: as very distinct identities. Like me, the reader has to *both* remember and put aside the awareness that this is one woman, whose life experience has shattered her into many parts. The current state of the field now supports the approach I took, that the individual identities must be dealt with directly for any progress to be made.

Emma introduced me to the world of dissociation and multiplicity. She was my teacher as well as my patient. Together we learned how to deal with her many selves and how to help her grow more whole and more stable. In the 90s when I started the work with Emma, my professional community did not readily recognize MPD (DID) as a legitimate diagnosis. The phenomenon of dissociation was frequently overlooked and under-treated; this might still be true. Although some psychiatrists were writing about both the phenomena and the treatment, this work was not widely read by clinicians; this also might still be true.

Mild dissociation is a universal phenomenon. Some common examples are highway hypnosis where one drives correctly and safely, but without conscious attention; daydreaming; or blanking out for a moment in a normal conversation. In the context of trauma, dissociation is a last ditch attempt to deal with overwhelming experience. Dissociation has been likened to a circuit breaker for the nervous system. If the psychic and/or physical pain or the anguish of betrayal and neglect are too much, an individual can pull the plug and go "offline" by separating sensation in the body from consciousness, going numb, or dampening emotion. In the case of DID, "offline" becomes an identity: Emma, who suffered repeated sadistic rapes and heart shredding betrayals, became Louie. She believed Louie could be tougher and more resilient because he was a boy.

Through my long and intense work with Emma, I came to understand and admire the genius of an adaptation that allows a child to survive betrayal, cruelty, suffering, torture, chaos and neglect by dividing the mind. Emma, like so many others like her, carved her unimaginable suffering into manageable pieces.

In this memoir, I introduce several of the major characters in Emma's inner world. They struggled to be known by me and to stay safe at the same time. The workings of memory are important in understanding traumatic experience and survival, so a discussion of memory is included. In addition to the major characters, the reader will be introduced to Emma's spirit guides: aspects of herself that she experienced as existing in another dimension, unlike all her other part-selves, or ego states, as I often call them in this book. They were key to her survival and strongly influenced our work together. The drama and the mutual caring that developed between us in this intense and long term work is an important part of this story.

Over time I came to easily identify "switches" as Emma shifted from one ego state to another. Louie, Eve, Missy or any of the others would either announce their presence when there was a switch from Emma, or I learned to discern very subtle shifts in posture, facial tone, vocal timbre, the way they held their shoulders. The youngest child parts often sat on the floor or turned their toes inward the way young children do.

I use the term "ego state" to refer to the "parts" or "sub-personalities" within Emma. An ego state is an organized system of behavior and experience whose elements are bound together; in Emma's case, into separate identities. I refer to my own ego states as well, which are not separate identities but nonetheless are a set of behaviors and feelings that cohere and vary from situation to situation.

I have seasoned the tale with bits of my own history, as well as what it was like to be Emma's therapist and how my own ego states were recruited and grew within the crucible of our work. Although Emma's functioning and segmenting of identities keeps her on the extreme end of a continuum, I occupy a place on that continuum as well. All human beings do. Almost everyone has had to deal with more than they were developmentally able to at one time or another: divorce, death or illness in the family, the absence of one or more parents, family dysfunction, emotional, physical and/or sexual abuse are just a few examples. Any event or events that overwhelm an individual can produce traumatic effects. That is the very definition of trauma.

The treatment was moderately successful in that Emma achieved a high degree of co-operation among her various identities. Some identities integrated into a larger whole, leaving a smaller, more stable group who could co-ordinate their activities. The outcome was not perfect, however. There are still unresolved issues for Emma and her cohort.

I recently watched the 1957 film "Three Faces of Eve," prompted by the death of Christine Sizemore, the woman portrayed in the film. Both the book, written by her first psychiatrists, and the film captured the public imagination and were blockbusters, earning a young Joanne Woodward an Academy Award. The story of three very separate identities living within one individual—Eve White, Eve Black, and Jane—took turns upon the stage, doing and undoing Ms. Sizemore's life.

I was struck by how dated the film was and how crude the techniques employed in helping Eve. Well, it *was* 1957. We have learned so much in the intervening decades about trauma, dissociation, the fascinating phenomena of what was known to Eve's psychiatrists as Multiple Personality Disorder, and most importantly, about its treatment.

Upon reflection, though, I remembered that the line given to the psychiatrist, "We really don't know much about Multiple Personalities," was not true, or shouldn't have been true. Eve's psychiatrists seemed only dimly aware that the phenomena that she was manifesting were rooted in childhood trauma. About 70 years earlier, Pierre Janet was working and writing in France about dissociation, the division of consciousness into discrete states, and listening to patients in his clinics tell him what was on their minds. Unfortunately Janet's clinical discoveries were overshadowed by his contemporary Sigmund Freud and Freud's followers. Freud initially embraced the traumatic source of the dissociative states he saw in his patients, but later disavowed this thesis.

Janet's main papers were not translated into English until 1989. The foremost scholar of traumatic states and their psychological consequences was essentially unknown to English speaking psychiatrists and psychotherapists until almost 1990. Bessel van der Kolk and Onno van der Hart, both European-born psychiatrists, were instrumental in raising consciousness in the U.S. of Janet's work. Nearly a century earlier, Janet had treated many patients with sequestered identities and described them in detail. Some scholars in the field have speculated that it was and is our tendency to both recoil from and disavow the reality of child abuse, particularly the *sexual* abuse of children that has contributed to this historical amnesia.

Multiple Personality Disorder is now designated as Dissociative Identity Disorder (DID). At the time of the film, this phenomenon was thought to be a very rare and highly aberrant occurrence. At present it is estimated that *at least* 2% of the general population meets the criteria for DID; this is slightly more than schizophrenia and slightly less than bipolar disorder. More than likely, DID is under-diagnosed as it is by nature a hidden condition and not readily disclosed by those afflicted. Additionally, many clinicians are not adequately trained in identifying DID and will only discern it in the most florid of presentations.

Ms. Sizemore's obituary indicates that "Eve" was not cured by her original psychiatrists as implied in the book and movie. Furthermore, there were a good deal more than three manifestations of Eve's fractured identity. Years later, more expert and informed treatment helped her to attain stability in her life and reportedly a thorough integration of as many as 22 personalities in all.

Since 1957 we have come to know a great deal more about dissociation. We currently understand Dissociative Disorders as an acute variant of chronic Post Traumatic Disorder, the consequence of severe childhood abuse.

Dealing with the skepticism of lay and professional people is part of the experience of every therapist treating DID. This is true of allegations of sexual abuse in general. In the '90s when I started with Emma, this was even more the case than it is now. DID *does* seem like magic; the ability to hide aspects of your personality from yourself and others and grow discrete identities from this process is wondrous. However, there is nothing like sitting with an individual with this capacity and experiencing it directly to convert skepticism to awe: consider the case of Cliff and his dog.

Cliff, a young man with DID whom I treated long after I met Emma, brought his dog to therapy sessions every week. Cliff's dog was very well trained, a lovely mutt named Alf. When the adult Cliff was present, usually at the beginning of a session, he would always instruct Alf to sit quietly in the waiting room, the door slightly ajar so he would not disturb our process or become upset with changes that Cliff might go through. Alf, ever obedient, stayed out of sight in the waiting room. But as soon as the adult Cliff switched to a child self-state, Alf nosed the door open and moved into the office, nuzzling "Cliffie," a younger part-self of the adult Cliff. Alf would *never* have done this as long as the adult was present. Alf could not see Cliff from where he lay, nor could he see me, so he could not detect even a subtle shift in posture. He did not hear the child self-state because Cliffie didn't speak right away, nor did I. Although out of sight, Alf somehow sensed the change and acted accordingly. Cliffie would not chastise him and more than likely, Cliffie would need the comfort of a nuzzle at the moment Alf came in the room.

Whatever sense Alf possessed, we undoubtedly possess as well in a diminished form, and it is that doggie sense that knows with uncanny certainty that "someone else is here now." Therapists may or may not be trained to refine this sense, to pay attention to hunches, to resonance, to something activated in the body; so subtle identity switches are not always recognized. I have heard therapists say, *"Every time the client came in, it was as if she was a completely different person, it was very hard to get a bead on things."* My response: *"Well, it's possible she was present in a different self-state each time, and that's why you are bewildered. In a way, she was a different person."* Without the paradigm of DID embedded in awareness therapists, we may miss this. We are not always as sharp as Alf.

Frank Putnam, the wonderfully wise and compassionate psychiatrist whose book on treating Multiple Personality Disorder I read feverishly over a weekend following the revelation of Emma's diagnosis, said of former MPD doubters who encountered their first patient with this condition that they often responded as if they had made a unique discovery. "My first response [to them] is that they are now cursed—to see it again and again but none of their colleagues will ever believe them."

Ego states, self-states, sub-personalities, splits or parts differ in many, sometimes amazing ways. Different ego states may have different wardrobes, different handwriting. One part may dress provocatively; another will dress to be invisible. If they have friends, the parts may have different friends and some parts may have no friends. One part may be artistic, one a good speller, another an avid reader. They may even have different allergies or respond differentially to medications and medical procedures. You will learn later that some of Emma's self-states needed glasses, some did not. There are boy "parts" and girl "parts, adult parts and child parts. Some ego states are heterosexual, some bisexual or homosexual. Most importantly, ego states contain different affects, differing emotional qualities. Some of Emma's states were very angry, even scary at times. Some were cheerful and adventurous, some sweet, shy, bookish, thoughtful and loving.

Individuals with this condition are often accused of faking it, seeming like they are play-acting switches between identities. Maybe this is occasionally true. But for the most part, multiple identities are hidden and only emerge when there is a degree of safety in a relationship. In the interests of self-protection, Emma's system moved slowly and carefully before exposing its fractures. It took a year for Emma to reveal to me that she had multiple identities.

There is neurological evidence to validate switches. Functional MRI's are devices that can track changes in blood flow in the brain and thus neuronal activation in real time. There have been explorations with individuals diagnosed with DID who can switch identities upon request. The fMRI results are remarkable. At the instance of a switch, different areas of the brain light up. This is not true for controls who are just pretending or acting.

Dissociative Identity Disorder is real. It is the marker for extreme suffering and it is truly awe-inspiring to witness.

chapter 3
"when I was a boy"

I won't forget when Peter Pan came to my house, took my hand
I said I was a boy; I'm glad he didn't check.
I learned to fly, I learned to fight
I lived a whole life in one night
We saved each other's lives out on the pirate's deck...

When I was a boy, I scared the pants off of my mom,
Climbed what I could climb upon
And I don't know how I survived,
I guess I knew the tricks that all boys knew.
And you can walk me home, but I was a boy, too.
— "When I Was a Boy," lyrics by Dar Williams

It was exactly a year into the treatment, a time of floundering and frustration for us both, when Emma and I shared a watershed moment. On this day, Emma handed me a letter written in her handwriting addressed to her father; a letter she seemed puzzled to have found lying around. It was a letter of accusation, a brief against his criminal behavior towards her and a sketch of the progression of that behavior from the time she was 4 years old onward. She writes that at age 10:

...the nightmares began. Your drinking was out of control. You were abusing everybody in the family. There wasn't anybody to turn to for help. It was too painful to live in the external world with you, so she [sic] went inside to live in an internal world where it was always safe.

...You might have gotten the 'body' but you didn't get the 'mind.' It went to sleep when the tears stopped coming. Changes started happening, she became something else that was numb, unfeeling, uncaring, un-needing of anyone...(It is safe to live in the blackness of your own mind when you close your eyes you can't see anything and when you open them you can't see anything, so there is nothing to fear)...

The awakening has begun. There are many different levels of feelings about what you have done.... The mind is a keeper of many parts. I am told that this is a survival mechanism and can begin to accept that.

As of right now, I feel like a grenade went off inside of me and there are pieces everywhere. Some of those pieces inspired me to write this. It [is] my job to put them back together.

Emma was in her late 20s when we met, I in my 40s. She was androgynous in appearance, slight, usually dressed neatly in jeans and a t-shirt. Hesitant, shy and soft-spoken, there was something unidentifiable about Emma that drew me to her, and it wasn't the story, which it often was with me, because there wasn't much of a story to begin with.

Emma had always been vague about both her history and her symptoms. Her major complaint was depression, but the description of her depression was rather nebulous. I was later to learn that she had a great deal of trouble sleeping: nightmares and night terrors were a constant problem for her. Eating was also a chore; she was thin and would get thinner during times of crisis. There were certain textures in foods that she could not abide and she was plagued by unexplained vomiting episodes. She could not account for periods of time during an average day.

Emma had small children, an infant daughter and a son several years older. An earlier treatment had failed to get off the ground. The welfare of the new baby was an important motivating factor in her attempting treatment with me. Her motivation was not so clear at the outset, but became obvious later in our process: she wanted her new baby to have a better childhood than her firstborn whom she had sometimes neglected, sometimes abused. To let herself come to therapy when she had so many fears and so many secrets to protect was an act of love and courage on Emma's part.

Her parents were still alive and she was terrified of her father. Both parents lived several hundreds of miles away and she did not see much of them. She halfway believed her father had magical powers and would know what she was sharing with me. She had been told this as a child, so as never to break the seal of secrecy. It was clear that she hated her father, feared him and avoided him. She seemed to be more connected to her mother, but it was a fraught and ambivalent connection.

The first year of our working together was a strange one. There was no hint of multiplicity, of dissociative states. Emma's affect was flat, vacuous. In retrospect, her blankness was a clue, but I was untrained and clueless myself at the time. She alluded to a history of being sexually abused by her violent and alcoholic father, but could offer very little information about this. She had been referred by a mentor, a teacher of hers who knew of the abuse and had more or less interviewed me on the phone to make sure I was the right person for Emma. Again, the counseling center had pointed to me as the "expert." I think the mentor knew of the "parts," the ego states that were separate one from the other within Emma, and she wanted to make sure I could handle this, but she did not share this information with me at that time. Maybe I wouldn't have signed on had I known and truly understood what this meant.

The letter above appeared at the end of the first year of treatment. In the letter, Emma laid it all out for me. She spoke of herself in the third person, she alluded to parts that need to be re-connected, there are at least two different styles of penmanship and yet…I didn't get it. I didn't consciously understand that Emma had many inner selves, identities that stood separate from the "host" Emma who presented herself to me in our weekly sessions. Perhaps prompted by an unconscious comprehension, I started using "parts" language.

Emma was strangely disconnected from the letter, as if it weren't *she* that had written it. I said something like, "Some part of you is extremely angry with your father, and for good reason. Right now you don't feel so connected to that angry part."

Suddenly there was a change: the currents in the air shifted, a goose-bumpy sensation all over my body. Neck hair tingly, my skin knew immediately something really important was happening. It was as if a part of me, *not* the more conscious, linguistic and thinking part, recognized the shift a few split seconds before full awareness kicked in. Without introduction, a 10-year-old boy sat across from me in place of Emma, the 28-year-old woman. A slight change in posture and facial expression hardly noticeable to the eye, but known to the rest of me: a child was now sitting across from me, the mischievous, appealing, fun-loving Louie. Emma had "switched."

"Hi, I'm Louie." Now I knew why she had always been blank, empty, vague. Emma was only one "part" of the whole. Her trauma had been so severe that she had sectioned off parts of herself. Louie was one of those "parts," one of those ego states, one of those alternative selves of the greater Emma.

Louie was vivid, full of beans, and often trouble. Louie held a lot of Emma's life energy. His entrance into the therapy, after a year of mostly nothing happening, marked the beginning of forward, sometimes chaotic and inexplicable movement.

In later years I would recognize the switches rather quickly without so much drama, but this was the first time. I like to think that I did not look shocked, that my outside did not look much like my insides, which were shaking. But I was awake, very awake.

Louie

The boy, Louie, had more of their story than Emma. He knew what had happened to her, or at least some of it, and he supplied a lot of the missing pieces. Over time he became the gateway to other part selves, alternative selves who, like him, held a few or a lot of the fractured puzzle pieces of Emma's history. Much of the trouble that Emma got into, multiple speeding tickets, bumps and bruises and even deep cuts on her body that she could never account for, were his handiwork.

Louie was always trying to get Emma's attention, to tell her some of the story of their lives. "She won't listen to me, she never listens. That's why I cut her," he told me in the weeks to come. The physical injuries were his doing, although he consistently denied that they shared a body! It was her body that bled, not his.

Emma did not want to listen to the memories or even to acknowledge that Louie was there. Louie told me that she tried to block him out and/or ignore him. But *I* listened, riveted. Through my recognizing, acknowledging and really *seeing* him, Louie was able to change, to stop speeding, to stop endangering their lives, to stop the cutting and hurting. Over a *very* long period of time, Louie grew up and his age and life stage actually changed. As I write this, Louie is now an adult, the same age as Emma, and pretty much CEO of Emma's system of part-selves. Initially it seemed he created the chaos. Now, after many years of treatment, he is more likely to try to co-ordinate and collaborate.

Louie, and other part-selves, had always been isolated from the outside world. Emma only knew Louie. She had heard him from early childhood. "He always wears a torn and dirty T- shirt," she described with disgust that first day. What Emma saw inside her head was a messy 10-year-old scamp.

Louie knew several of the others I was to learn about. There was a rich inner world for each part: landscapes, rooms, dissimilar appearances, different names, clothing, interests…all cut off from the outer world. At the beginning of the treatment there didn't seem to be a lot of interaction between these sub-personalities or self-states. That was going to be the work of the therapy: fostering both communication and collaboration among them.

The mere fact of my seeing Louie, as Louie, changed him: he was now engaged in a social context, activating a part of his brain never before activated. If he interacted with someone on the outside, which he did quite a bit as Emma grew up, it was not as "Louie," but as a beard, a front for Emma. Louie emerged when Emma could not manage a situation because of pain, shame or terror. Emma had believed as a child that being a boy was a protection against abuse; she thought her older brother had not been sexually abused. Although he had been repeatedly physically and emotionally brutalized by Emma's father, she had a belief that "Boys are stronger. Boys are brave. Boys can't be raped."

I experienced Louie as real. Really real. There was no question that this was not play-acting. Emma had divided herself for protection and Louie was the first, and the most persistent of these divisions.

Emma—the presenting adult Emma—was initially aghast, bewildered, frightened, and finally relieved when I explained to her that I thought she had many partitioned selves, that I believed she could properly be diagnosed as having Multiple Personality Disorder (MPD), the diagnostic designation at that time. "I thought I was schizophrenic, hearing voices. I always heard Louie." Emma's supposition is actually common, or at least it was common at the time. Schizophrenia is a psychosis characterized by hallucinations, delusions, disorganized thinking and usually a passivity and apathy. Emma exhibited none of these symptoms. She heard Louie's voice, maybe she could see him, but when I addressed him, he spoke back. That is not a characteristic of a true hallucination; hallucinations do *not* chat with outsiders. When Louie was present, Emma was not. If I asked to speak with Louie, he came forward and Emma receded. This is *not* true in schizophrenia. The segregation of identities was complete with Emma.

The diagnosis of MPD was frightening to her, but it also made sense. As I got a grasp on the diagnosis myself, I was able to explain to her that it was a reasonable, creative psychological solution to the great suffering and psychological injury she had suffered as a child. The diagnosis of MPD accompanies almost certainly a history of early, repetitive, sadistic trauma and almost always sexual abuse.

I have been re-reading *Anne of Green Gables*, a book I adored as a child. Anne is an orphan and arrives on Prince Edward Island at the age of 11, where she is adopted by a middle-aged childless couple.

Before this, she has had a very rough childhood, neglected and if not physically abused, certainly emotionally abused. She longs for a "bosom friend," an intimate to whom she can confide her feelings and thoughts. Anne—bright, heroically imaginative and endlessly optimistic—creates a friend from her reflection in the glass pane of an empty bookcase.

> *I called her Katie Maurice, and we were very intimate. I used to*
> *talk to her by the hour, especially on Sunday, and tell her every-*
> *thing. Katie was the comfort and consolation of my life. (P.58)*

Emma, whose suffering far exceeds Anne's, has done something similar, but Emma's friend comes unbidden, automatically, and she does not know that this a work of her artful imagination and more importantly, the urgent need to survive.

When in the presence of DID, the parts are clear and real. When a child part appears, there is no question that the adult, or "host," is no longer present. Clinicians who have never knowingly worked with DID so often question that this is so and ascribe delusion to the therapist who is working with these individuals.

Usually we lose our younger selves as we grow. We might be able to momentarily recapture a child state, prompted by photos, stories, smells, tastes, usually something that prompts sense memory. For all intents and purposes, more integrated folks do not have magical access to the child states that people with serious dissociative disorders have. We lose our childhoods as part of the deal we make with maturity. This is not so for the individual who has experienced severe trauma and is fixated at various points in childhood. The self-states are living memorials to intense suffering. Louie once said, "We moved the soul around so they wouldn't get us, wouldn't murder our souls." In so doing they preserved some of the life force of childhood as well.

This ability to dissociate is both a curse and a gift in a fractured self. The curse may be obvious: life is terribly disrupted if you leave the present moment completely when triggered by some threat or imagined threat. Learning, working, loving, raising children become chaotic with shifting self-states. For instance, a 10-year-old boy driving your car can get speeding tickets and get your license suspended. More ominously. very angry, violent ego states can be activated by demanding young child part. There is a gift, however: the child witness that survived and can tell the story that needs to be told in order to heal the adult.

Years after treatment ended, I sent this chapter to Louie to review. He wrote:

> *I was scared of you, and I was so small. Something about the way you looked at me and you did not judge me. It drew me to you. I had never felt that kind of emotion, and you did seem to like me?...but at the time I did not fully trust that you were not going to harm me? I remember testing you and you passed every time. I thought is there really people that care? [Angel, a spiritual guide inside] embraced me and told me to go be with you and I did. I always consulted him with questions...is this real I asked him? He said 'do you feel it.' I answered yes! He held me and I said I told you there are good people out there and you must trust what you feel. So I did.* ☺

The theory of treatment, at least the one that I followed as I sought to help Emma reclaim and unite shards of her many "parts," is much like Rabbi Luria's concept of uniting the shards of light that make up the mystical universe. Integration and unity represent the ultimate healing. I was to learn, however, that often the best I could do was to facilitate communication, building friendly and cooperative links between all of Emma's "parts."

Not all DID patients are as likeable and as intensely engaging as Emma was, but many are. All of the part-selves are terrified children trying bravely to cope with unimaginable, extreme abuse. Their emotional lives are intense, everything is hyper-real. Many are naturally drawn to suffering children. At least therapists are. And I was.

chapter 4
angel

"My work is finished and your work is only beginning.
Don't be afraid to love May.
She won't let you go until it is time to fly free on your own wings.
The search for someone to trust is over. It's your time to tell."
—Angel

About a year into our work together this message was delivered to Emma from Angel, a spiritual guide who had been with her since childhood. Emma told me that Angel had seen her through many unbearable experiences that can only be described as terroristic acts: pitiless beatings, brutal rapes, torture at the hands of her father and his friends. These acts were meant to terrify and control, and they did. Emma insisted that Angel was not a part or an ego state, a derivative of her suffering, but rather a guiding light that existed entirely outside of herself and had always been there. Angel did not have direct contact with Emma but heard about him only through Louie.

I found among my messy, fragmented, but voluminous case notes of Emma a picture of Angel, drawn by one of the parts who was an artist and did drawings of all of Emma's parts at one time or another. I

Angel

couldn't really tell from the picture if Angel was male or female, but I had always assumed that Angel was male. In the drawing, Angel's figure is outlined in yellow; he sprouts modest wings on his back. He is gazing down with concern, comforting a very small, maybe four-year-old child who is sleeping. Tears slip down the child's face.

This poem appears underneath the title, "The Unseen Warrior":

> *For Angel our unseen warrior*
> *Our brother and friend*
> *Who for our safety we depend*
> *We ask you now to come defend our precious frightened soul*
>
> *We know you've been here all along*
> *And will remain our whole life long*

But with this simple childish prayer
We ask you please to help us be strong

Sometimes at night we do awaken
Let us not feel fear forsaken
To every saint your visit paid
You always said 'Don't be afraid.'

Many years later, when Angel had faded away, other spiritual guides appeared accompanying Joey, a younger version of Louie who demonstrated rather convincing clairvoyance. The guides spoke to Joey with wisdom directives that he frequently ignored, eventually banishing them from consciousness. Both Angel and these later spirit guides always supported the treatment and so I supported them and never questioned their reality.

As I think back on Angel now, I wonder if this attachment to a wise, loving comforter and guide experienced as a *real* outside entity kept the capacity for loving attachment alive within Emma. In a way, it is a solution to a serious dilemma. Attachment to another human is key to human survival; without it we literally die. But when all the caretakers are plainly dangerous, a threat to survival, creating figures within oneself as resources is an inspired adaptation. The pattern for attachment shaped by early experiences endures throughout the lifespan. It is not absolutely fixed, thankfully, and can be modified by later life experiences, such as a long term and beneficial psychotherapy or a loving adult partnership, but the shape of things begins in childhood. Emma said more than once, "As a child, all I needed was a crumb, a crumb of caring and it sustained me for a bit." Maybe Angel was the representation of that "crumb," writ large.

I don't really know who wrote the poem above but I would guess it was a group of ego states that collaborated for this purpose. That would happen from time to time, a blending of several parts to accomplish a specific goal.

Many, many years later, Emma hinted that Angel may have been the representation of a part of the real mother, an elusive part that was spiritual and loving and wanted to keep them safe. Protecting Emma was perilous for Emma's mother: the father would have abused her brutally had he known. In secret, *actually* in the basement, she taught her children lessons about Christianity and the beneficence of a savior. These lessons stopped when Emma was under seven years old or so.

Mother was probably as fractured in her being as Emma, suffering from the same disorder and even teaching Emma how to dissociate and create parts with alternative identities. I deduced this from various hints Emma dropped over the years. Emma's mother repeatedly and disastrously failed to keep her children safe, but she seemed to have had a sliver of self that believed in a benevolent Deity, and she tried to deliver Emma into the hands of a messenger of that Deity.

Emma's mother witnessed beatings, rapes, and grotesque punishments of both of her children and seemed helpless to intervene. Emma told me, "One time she left me alone with him for days. She took Johnnie with her. Dark Daddy (that's what she called him) was dead drunk, threatening, and violent. I don't remember quite what happened but I was soooo scared. I thought she was never coming back."

The mother seemed to have elected to protect Emma's older brother and took the chance that at six or seven years old, Emma would survive. And at least, physically, she did.

Through Angel, Emma held on to some hope for the existence of goodness and compassion in a world that was profoundly unsafe for her and devoid of those qualities. Angel also helped *me* to hope, to believe that Emma could heal and become less chaotic, more functional.

I wondered aloud to Louie: "Could Angel come in to talk to me?" "Not really" he explained, "Angel only speaks to me." One time, however, Angel *was* present to Emma when she was in my office. She described him as having a very soothing, special voice. I found this in my notes for I did not remember it. Mostly I would only get reports of an encounter from Louie. This one time he manifested to Emma in my presence and she described him as "having a perfect voice that emerged from his Adam's apple." His voice, his presence was "suffused with warmth." Emma asked me if I felt the warmth as she did. I had to admit that I did not. But I did see that Emma was profoundly moved by what she was feeling: her face softened, she breathed deeply, her characteristic wariness slid off her for the moment. Angel was "a super good" father who told her she was doing a great job by working in therapy.

Louie, or the adult Emma, told me that Angel explained the system of multiple parts to Emma, describing their function and how each was created. I didn't always know where information like this was coming from and it didn't help the therapy to necessarily chase that down in every case. Suffice to say that Angel lifted amnestic barriers so that all the parts could tell me the story of their life. Ordinarily the barriers were air-tight. Neither Emma nor any outsider could know the story of their chilling childhood.

As indicated in the quote at the start of this chapter, Angel decided that his helper role had to diminish in order for Emma and particularly for Louie—who had the strongest connection to Angel—to turn to me and entrust me with their story. This was an important shift, maybe the first gesture toward an attachment to an "outside" real, earthly relationship. Angel retreated but did not actually disappear. Occasionally he would show up to comfort and support Emma/Louie in moving forward with the treatment, to encourage "a leap of faith."

Angel's "message board" was often a dream. There was an actual leap-of-faith dream in which Louie jumped over a great distance onto my front porch. This was Angel's metaphoric encouragement to hang in with the treatment, although it was arduous and painful. Angel wasn't always the "winner" though. In this case, Emma did drop out for a time.

By recognizing and accepting Angel as a "real" spirit, not another part, I sought to strengthen his function as a stabilizer, an internal helper. It turned out I was strengthening something in myself as well. I believe my own capacity for containing mystery and making room for spiritual possibilities grew as a result of the work I was doing with Emma and others. The existence of a spiritual being/part self,

an inclination toward both clairvoyance and a strong sense of the
transcendent is quite common in individuals like Emma who have
been overwhelmed as young children by extreme trauma. Angel helped
Emma to survive.

This is what Louie had to say about Angel, many years later, when
he and Emma were middle-aged adults. I have not changed Louie's
punctuation. It's the way he writes.

> (Angel) was very real to me and I still can't explain where he
> came from? How could I, a fractured 10 year old boy make him
> up? He had wisdom and compassion that I never received from
> a living person? He was not from this earthly plane. He was
> from a source of light and love. I do recall him coming to me at
> times of extreme abuse and saying "close your eyes baby," and I
> did. I didn't feel any of it? I knew it happened but even to this
> day I do not remember any pain or visual recall of what actually
> happened? It's not important to me to have the memory, just
> that feeling of being hugged and taken away from reality. I[f]
> that sounds a bit crazy, but it's how I remember it, and history
> is in the mind of the teller.

Holding my mind open for Emma and her belief in the divine origin
of Angel helped me to grow into a reasonably competent therapist with
highly traumatized individuals. The equivalent of "Angel" seemed to
exist in several patients with whom I was to work later on. I never felt
that I had to dispute Angel's *real* existence and what he meant to Emma.

In the early years of this treatment, when Angel was very much
around, there were two transformative experiences of my own in which
Angel probably had a hand. The first was my response to the death
of a younger cousin a few months shy of her 40th birthday. A healthy
woman with no disease, she died as a consequence of a medical error
during a routine procedure. She was in a coma for a few months but
despite pleadings and prayers by her family there was never any hope
she would wake up. My cousin had been very present in my own
childhood and her senseless death was devastating to me and to the

entire family. On some level it still is. I felt very alone during that time, geographically separated from my entire family, my husband travelling in Japan, my kids far away. A close friendship had recently dissolved as well.

Nothing about what had happened made sense. I couldn't wrap my head around it. There was no meaning in the suffering of her parents, sisters, husband and the terrible loss of an intensely lived life.

My cousin was a petite powerhouse, adorable, brilliant, creative, a devotee of family connection. She was without doubt the best cook and the most generous entertainer in our family. Her wedding was both lavish and great fun. She left a big hole in our small family. I can't say quite how, but the mystery of Angel offered me something during that bleakness. Angel could not rescue Emma during the worst of times but promised that there would be a time when she could and would be safe. Things would get better. Maybe that was the most important message Angel had to deliver…for both of us.

Looking back, I think that having these periodic communications from Angel, having Angel work with me to help the child parts of Emma, woke up in me a long slumbering spiritual impulse. Angel was a powerful force; his energy radiated beyond me to the peer supervision group that accompanied me on the Emma journey. As I reported on this case to my peer group and sought their counsel and support, they felt the awe and the mystery right along with me. Angel seemed so wise, so wholesome, it did seem credible to all of us that he was the "light, the spark" that had helped Emma endure.

When my cousin died I remembered my own childish faith, something I clung to in darkness as a child. During that difficult time, I regained access that child self, a spiritual connection that had sustained me once and could do so again. My own "Angel" took a turn upon the stage and I was comforted.

The second transformative experience related to Angel followed about a year later when I was invited to participate in a weekend workshop led by an Israeli woman who had come to teach Kabbalah and

Kabbalistic meditation. Kabbalah is a Jewish mystical tradition considered fringy by some and profound by others. I really didn't understand
what I was getting into but I got into it anyway. For three days, during
a time when I could ill afford three days out of my life, I sat and was
led in meditation and instruction by a woman who spoke poor English
but somehow made herself understood. I had met her briefly when she
lived in the US a few years before and I was so impressed by what I can
only call her "light," her intellectual brilliance and something beyond
the intellect, that I enrolled in the class. My back hurt, I doubted I could
sit that long and my dissertation was due a few months from then, but I
signed on. I think knowing and being instructed by "Angel" was a factor
in my willingness to go, and again, hold my mind open.

It proved transformative. Shosh's "light" became real brilliance in
that workshop: not the smart kind, the spiritual kind. I learned how to
meditate, at least a particular method of meditation. She had us seek a
"higher self," or a soul. Like Angel, she carried within her an energy that
radiated to those around her; a guru-like loving vibrancy that brought
out the best in everyone. People who get close to the Dalai Lama or
Thich Nhat Hanh describe a similar experience. I felt myself to be my
truest self, or best self, around Shosh. She (like the Dalai Lama) was and
is an adherent of the transmigration of souls: reincarnation. Through
meditation, she believes you can connect with the essential self/soul that
is reincarnated infinitely. Once connected to that higher self, there is a
guidance that one can sense in one's life.

I don't know how much I can buy into Shosh's way of seeing the
world, the higher self and eternity, but once again I find that keeping
my mind and my being open feels right, feels good, feels like growth.
What I learned from Emma, to be present with uncertainty, to suspend
judgment, served me well with Shosh, then and now.

A Reflection:
  Being able to accommodate, to remain open about experiences
  outside of one's direct experience seems to be a precondition for

trauma therapists. Either you come to the work with a high tolerance for ambiguity, you develop it as you practice, or, I believe, you become less effective with individuals like Emma. I did not need to know who Angel was, if he was celestial or a part like the other parts. Supporting his presence in our work moved us along. That was all that was important.

chapter 5
memory, the pond

I was in my early 20s. I stood with my mother in the side yard between our house—the house in which I grew up—and that of the new next-door neighbors, Katie and her family. My mother was dispensing advice to Katie, a lively young mother of three small children. Katie was a tall, twinkling, fun-loving, blue-eyed woman. She was telling my mother: "Sam has a nose for trouble. That pond scares me." Sam was about three, Katie's youngest. Both of our houses were perched above a vast marsh and a multi-acre pond that typically froze over in the winter. From our backyard and hers, there was a steep drop, a few stories down to Ware's Pond. My siblings and I skated there every winter before global warming and overzealous housing development pretty much did in that pristine area.

I had spent many years gazing at the pond from the picture window in our living room. As I write this, I realize I have had many, many dark dreams of that pond over the years, of swimming in the murky cold water, of swimming too far out, getting caught in a tidal wave, drowning. In waking life we never swam there, no one did. I always wondered how deep it was, how cold. As I looked back on this time, I started to dream of the pond again, the pond and the marsh, and symbolic representations of the many parts of myself embedded in the boggy banks.

Surrounding the pond was what we called "the swamp," a marshy, squishy, unwholesome mess that froze over in the winter. I never saw it as the "rich wildlife refuge" as the much diminished area is described today. Who knew of conservation areas? Rachel Carson's warnings in *Silent Spring* had yet to be written and read. But there *was* wildlife, at least huge snapping turtles, up to 12 inches across, that emerged from the murk periodically, ambling down the middle of our street. Harmless, but still worrying black garter snakes appeared in the yard fairly often.

My father was a builder and had designed and erected the houses on our street. No one with kids in the early 1950s would buy a house directly above the pond, considering it unsafe for young children, so my father and grandfather (also a builder) built houses for themselves there on the two unsellable lots. But now it was the late '60s, my grandfather had sold his house, and Katie and family had moved into it.

Katie feared for the safety of her very small children. My mother reported, "When my kids were little I was also scared of the pond. Herb [my little brother] was fearless. I told him that there was quicksand down there. 'Don't go down there, you'll get sucked in.'" She laughed. Inwardly, my jaw dropped. Quicksand. Sucking quicksand? Is there such a thing as quicksand on this continent? Regularly featured in Tarzan movies and cartoons, I remembered the bad guys could and would be swallowed up by it. Terrifying. In that moment my "fraidy-cat" child state came nose to nose with my adult understanding.

I do not actually remember my mother telling us this when we were little. I was seven, my brother only four when we moved to that house, my baby sister a month or two old. But I do remember the sickening feeling in the pit of my stomach when we descended the slope in our backyard in winter to go ice skating on the pond. Evidently we had been told it was safe in winter because the quicksand froze. There were always squishy places between the frozen patches that made me afraid, though. I never really knew why. My body remembered the warning, not my mind.

I was struck dumb when I heard my mother's words. There was really nothing dangerous in the marsh, but until that moment I had held, *unrevised,* a thoroughly preposterous idea that our swamp was a no man's land, something like the jungles in deepest, darkest Africa. My brother, for whom this fiction was created, was undeterred, by the way; he regularly went down there to forage and explore, and he got in trouble for it. Me? No way.

If anyone had asked me when I was older if there was quicksand in the marsh, I would have quickly concluded that this was a ridiculous notion. This ancient belief, however, although never fully surfacing, had influenced my behavior (I was never a good skater), my mood (anxiety), and my dreams. The memory had no chance to be revised until that moment with Katie, many years later. Childhood is a storehouse of unrevised memory that wouldn't hold water (pun intended) for a moment in an adult's estimation. Which is one very good reason, by the way, to enter psychotherapy!

Comedian Sarah Silverman's, older sister Susan has written a memoir, which includes a startling example of the paradox of unre-membered memory, i.e. traumatic memory. She describes the severe separation anxiety that she has had all of her life:

> It was a constant battle to be able to live my life without the people I loved in my sight…. Sometimes at school…into high school, I would need to be able to check in. I would need to be able to know that everyone was OK. There was such anxiety the whole day. I was so distracted by the possibilities of people dying that it was hard to focus…. I would look at other kids who are laughing, having lunch, doing their thing, and think, How can they be so carefree? How can they not be worried right now? (https://www.npr.org/2016/05/23/479150041/ susan-silverman-on-anxiety-adoption-and-making-a-family-in-an-uncertain-world)

Susan had been in therapy for two or three years when she mentioned to her therapist that her infant brother had died in his crib when she was two years old. The parents had been on vacation, the children in the care of grandparents when a collapsing crib had killed her brother. Her therapist was flabbergasted that she had never mentioned this before. Susan had discounted its influence because she had been so little and held no memory of the event. When the therapist connected her anxiety to this "unremembered" family trauma, Susan felt the dark cloud that had been with her forever literally "fly away." The anxiety was not completely gone, but some of its enormous weight had lifted.

I often use my quicksand anecdote with patients to convince them of the value of revisiting the past. In Emma's case that involved real horrors, not merely fictitious quicksand. But the frightening secrets buried in the discrete, even warring ego states called Louie, Eve, Nan and others yet to be discussed here needed to be revisited also in order to be revised. The message, the subtext of each horrendous memory was always "…and I was alone." The goal of the revision: "I survived. I am here now. I am not alone. I have children. I have a partner. I have friends. I have a therapist."

There are many paradigms that developmental psychology brings to the understanding of our minds. The one I have found most useful—and Emma taught me this—is the concept of multiple ego or self-states co-existing within each of us, not just in those with DID. Within every adult lurks a clutch of younger selves containing fears, biases, points of view, tastes and beliefs that are no longer relevant to the adult self. These ego states, in neurological terms, are bundles of neuronal connections that are linked together in patterns of information, affect, behavior and sensory states and are evoked together.

Most people would acknowledge that when they arrive at the beach, or at their family home, or at the scene of an unpleasant memory, certain feelings and certain behaviors come over them that are associated with that place, these people, that scene. That's an ego state or a self-state. Singer-songwriter Loudon Wainwright refers to what it is like to be an adult at the table with his family of origin, struggling to stay in his adult self state.

"Thanksgiving"
Let us somehow get through this meal
Without that bad old feeling
With history and memory
And home cooking we're dealing
Remind us that we are all grown up
Adults, no longer children
Now it's our kids that spill the milk
And our turn to want to kill them

The prayer, the appeal is "remind us that we are all grown up, adults, no longer children" because the child ego states step right up to the turkey and start feeling and perhaps acting like the child of old.

Stepping on a crack will not break your mother's back. There really are no monsters in the closet, and if there are, they are *you*. We know cracks will not break backs because we remember chanting that as kids; what we *don't* remember holds more sway. Misinformation stored in the unexamined ego states draws power from the shadows. Thus my anxiety about "the swamp."

It didn't take much for me to revise my estimation of the pond and the marsh. What was entirely unconscious became conscious in the light of reason and the "intervention" of the conversation with Katie, blew it all away. The child ego state that held the dread of the pond listened in; you might say, when the adult "me" got to examine the belief of sucking quicksand below our backyard, I could swiftly let it go.

It would be fair to say that this was an easy one, revising my dread of the pond and the swamp. More difficult are *ways of being* that are so embedded in my personality that transformation sometimes feels impossible. These ways of being are also a form of memory. One of my more severe difficulties, sometimes disguised as a strength, is a stubborn determination to transform that which is un-transformable. I am persistent. I don't give up easily. This may be an asset when learning how to play tennis. Working with Emma required a determination to hang in for a *very* long time: two decades. Another patient of mine

summed it up: "You are like a dog with a bone." And that has value…
sometimes. But, to mix metaphors shamelessly, I also tend to stay too
long at the fair.

I had a patient for many years who quit therapy three or four
times, always abruptly, with anger, always de-valuing me in the process.
Something like, "This is useless, you are useless," would accompany
the slammed door. Eventually she came and stuck it out, working hard
for many years. I think my enduring with her despite the multiple exits
and insults was the most meaningful intervention with her. She got
better. But when she asked me why I kept taking her back, I really had
no answer. I just couldn't quit.

This way of being is rooted in child ego states too. I struggled
long and hard against my father who, I felt, wanted to control the way
I thought. He always had to win. Not giving up on my point of view,
not giving in, was adaptive when I was young; I became dogged, which
was sometimes useful. The downside is I stay in relationships that don't
work, forever hoping that someday they will.

Emma splintered her identities to stay alive, to survive and not
completely disintegrate, to not go mad or even die of her psychic
wounds. My dogged ego states were adaptations to far less dire circumstances, but adaptations nonetheless.

My "doggedness" is a form of memory. There have been remarkable
developments in neuroscience that illuminate a lot about these ingrained
ways of being. We know there are different types of memory, different
storage areas in the brain for these different types, and very importantly
for its implications for psychotherapy, the brain is not fixed, it is open
to change.

Declarative or narrative or explicit memory refers to conscious
recall of people, places, objects, facts, and events. Implicit or procedural
memory is often embedded in the body, in our senses, in ways of being;
it is unconscious. We learn to ride a bike and forever remember to ride
the bike without thinking about it. My fear of the swamp had nothing
to do with remembering consciously what was told to me as a child, it

was just there in my "bones." If I'd remembered it explicitly I would likely have revised it long ago.

And then there is traumatic memory, which is of the implicit variety. Susan Silverman carries the memory of her baby brother's death by experiencing alarm whenever there is a separation from a loved one. But she has no cognitive memory of the event; just alarm. Although, like Emma, a trauma victim may have some of the story, most of the story is stored in the imagery system and the body. More or less concealed self-states hold the trauma. Flashbacks are good examples of this type of memory: there may be pictures and bodily sensations that are so vivid that there is no awareness of the present moment. The affected individual is embedded in the past moment of fear and horror.

What is unique to traumatic memory is that once stored, it does not get revised the way ordinary or declarative memory does. All the skepticism and even attack by memory researchers like Elizabeth Loftus on the validity of traumatic memory was based on the simple fact that ordinary memory is malleable; it is constructed and revised over time. Traumatic memory is implicit and is *not* revised over time.

Had there actually been quicksand in the boggy swamp of my childhood and had I been sucked into it barely escaping with my life, my "memories" of the event would be traumatic memories. More than likely they would be fragmentary. Whenever I would hike across a damp field or smell the characteristic smells of a marsh or catch sight of a snapping turtle I might have flashbacks, feel my limbs getting heavy and slow. I might feel a rush of terror, be flooded with adrenaline, break into a sweat and either flee the area or find myself frozen, rooted to the spot. If I didn't actually remember the event in a narrative, declarative manner the flashbacks might be even more intense.

If the imagined quicksand trauma had been followed by similar horrifying events, life- threatening events—perhaps engineered by someone who should have been trustworthy or beloved, like a family member or clergy—very separated self-states, such as we see in Emma, might well form. Trauma impacts brain structure and neural networks.

Our ability to know, reflect, and perceive ourselves are all adversely affected by trauma.

Emma partitioned and contained her horror memories within separate identities. I have sometimes called them parts here, as that is how discrete ego states, which have become alternate identities, are most often referred to in the professional literature. The parts take on lives of their own over time and as they are evoked over and over again in particular circumstances. For instance, Louie was considered to be a heroic boy, in the mold of Emma's idealized older brother, who could endure violence, pain and humiliation better than a mere girl, or so she imagined. Louie and virtually all the tougher crowd of ego identities were boys. As Louie was evoked many times in circumstances of terror, he took on a more solid existence. There were "splits" from Louie as well, boys who divided and then contained horrors that were even too much for Louie. The girl parts represented stresses associated with sexual abuse and loss. The system is actually more complex than this, but I have simplified matters here for the purposes of clarity.

Consider the genius of a system that divides horror into containable, *almost* manageable, fragments.

chapter 6
these are the twins

And then there were the twins: 13 years old when I first met them. One girl was shy, artistic, sad, ever-grieving. The other was hostile, aggressive, promiscuous, aligned with the abusers and dead-set against me and the therapy. I'm not sure why they are represented as twins within Emma's system, except perhaps to indicate that they were created at the same time, under similar circumstances.

Of course Emma always looked like Emma. Any fly on the wall would not have noticed any real change in appearance when one or the other of the twins was in the room, but in my mind's eye, even now as I reflect on my experience of them, I see them differently: Nan, the artistic twin, reluctant, eyes downcast, voice hesitant, clearly not happy to be in my office. She is soft, sweet, and shy. Eve, the other twin, is bold, sitting up straighter than Nan; she stares at me challengingly.

Nan came forward only when I specifically asked for her. "I'd like to get to know Nan." Emma left and shyly, Nan answered, "Why do you want to talk to *me*?" Once, when told that they all looked different inside, I was curious and I asked to see pictures of the different parts. Nan drew some very fine line drawings of each of the major "actors" at that time. She depicted Louie at age 10 with curly hair and blue eyes, smiling openly and easily. Another drawing represented Jet, an ego state with whom Louie would eventually blend, an unsmiling adolescent, tougher looking, his eyes tired and sad.

Occasionally Nan made sketches on behalf of the others; as the illustrator of the assembly, she would draw a feeling, an experience or a fantasy of one of the others. Louie asked her to create a picture of him fishing, with me looking serenely on in the background, a scene that represented and maybe partially satisfied his longing for a supportive maternal figure.

Nan, unlike her sister, was always quietly supportive of the treatment and seemed to trust me. She represented herself and her twin with the Yin/Yang symbol: a circle, half of which is dark with a dot of light, half, light with a dot of darkness.

When Emma's children were small, Nan took on mothering roles cuddling, cooking and caring for the kids when Emma was overwhelmed. She also mothered the younger part-selves within. "I make Mom's recipe of spaghetti and meatballs with homemade tomato sauce," a favorite sense memory from childhood. She was loyal to their mom and saw her more as a co-victim of the father than as an enabler or perpetrator: "Mom tried, but Dad hurt her too." There was a clear split inside between those parts who saw Emma's mother benignly and those who saw her as dangerous and a perpetrator herself.

Nan did friendship. Emma had had a dear friend when she was about 13 who had committed suicide. It was that friend who Nan endlessly mourned. Like so many who have been close to those who commit suicide, she felt guilty about surviving and going on with her life, painful as it was. During a period of treatment, Nan became friends with another woman in a therapy group that Sydney, my co-therapist, and I led for five years; that woman reminded her of the bygone bond.

As treatment progressed and Nan grew older, she grew bolder, less retiring, but I never saw a lot of her. Eventually she blended with other girl parts and was less distinct.

I am often asked how I knew when there was a "switch," when Emma was no longer there and Louie, or one of the twins, or someone else appeared. Of course, if they did not want me to know that there were these carefully partitioned parts, they could and did hide this. Eventually it was understood that I was permitted to observe Emma switching. There may have been a shift in posture or tone of voice that clued me in. The eyes were softer, or harder, but mostly it was a body feeling that was evoked in me, a felt sense, a visceral chill, and I knew something had changed. Attunement requires attention to the body, one's own and one's partner's, in relating. You can often *feel* some of what is going on with someone else: a slight tensing within, a change in breath or heartbeat, a chill or a flush, an ache, all clues.

Eve had all the markings of a bully. Inevitably she set me back on my heels. She confronted me: "You have no idea what you are doing; your blundering is dangerous! You have no idea what you are talking about and bad things will happen," she threatened. There was menace in her tone; it is clear she meant to intimidate me, and she did. In my mind's eye, she was covered in snarling tattoos. The Emma I knew as Emma was nowhere to be found when Eve was present. When Emma reappeared, she had no awareness that Eve had been talking to me and had threatened me.

"You are pathetic. You're playing with fire and you don't even know it." Now that I think back, there was an inherent contradiction in Eve's attacks on me. I am both powerful and useless; contemptible and dangerous, pitiful and a threat to Emma's stability, even her life. I wish I had seen the contradiction at the time! If I had it might have helped me, but I doubt that Eve would have been deterred in her attacks.

Eve can be understood as a kind of "cynical protector" of the system. Her intention was to keep everyone safe, and the untreated system seemed to her to be the safest solution to a profoundly unsafe childhood.

Eve did scare me. In treating Emma and all her parts, I always had to have one foot within the delusional world of multi part-selves, and one foot in my own reality as an adult, psychotherapist-observer. It was sometimes a struggle to remember that all Emma's parts were injured children. Eve had the ability to pull me with both feet into the delusional world. She was real and she could do me harm! Indeed, there was more to come.

Eve had aligned herself with the abusers to stay alive. If she was on their side and co-operated, Emma was more likely to survive; of course she was right and Emma *did* survive. Eve accepted the ideology of the abusers and didn't see it as mistreatment. She saw *me* as abusive. She was convinced, as many of the partitioned selves of Emma were, that the tormenters of her childhood were still around and had the ability to hurt them and me. Talking to me broke the seal of secrecy that as young children they had repeatedly been told meant death. Eve's reality was frozen in the past; she believed the danger was still forthcoming. At times *I* even felt the hot breath of these ghosts of the past on the back of my neck, so convincing was Eve.

I am reminded of a description of the dissociation of body parts that is the consequence of leprosy. Before there was a cure for the disease, it was understood that nerves died in the extremities of the victim. Afflicted limbs no longer felt pain. Evidently pain is an important part of the experience of self. No longer feeling pain, lepers neglected their limbs, failed to care for them, inadvertently injuring and "insulting" them, disfigurement ensued. Part of the treatment early on was to teach patients to care for themselves, to reclaim the "discarded" parts of their bodies. This perfectly describes, in the broadest outline, what Emma needed to do to heal. She needed to reclaim discarded parts of herself: Louie, Nan, even Eve. More than likely there was less resistance to doing this with lepers than with Dissociative Disorders! With Emma and others like her, there is a deep investment in the separation. What was designed for safety is not easily given up.

Therapists are the first line of caring. The therapist's task, perhaps not unlike the leper doctor, is to care for all the ego states and child selves, and to model empathy. Eve was the way she was because hers was an expedient, maybe even a brilliant response to brutal treatment—not unlike becoming one of the gang to protect oneself from gangs. The problem is of course that Eve, having survived the gang, believes they are still a threat to her. The gang has gone inside and she is still a member of the gang.

An important part of my job, like the leprosy doctor, is to care for the discarded "limbs" like Eve. It is not helpful to try to exile the difficult ones to make the therapist's life easier...although one is tempted.

Once when I was being menaced by Jet—a really scary part, even scarier than Eve—I hypnotically suggested that he go on "vacation," away from the main action. What a mistake! He came back loaded for bear and was even more menacing than before: "How dare you!" he growled.

Unhappily, Eve was very dug in. I was never able to fully connect with her. She did not come forward often or confront me directly. She worked behind the scenes, wreaking havoc when she could. It took a year or two for this to become more evident. To stretch the leper analogy, the Eve "limb" would not abide my care.

Eve represented the anti-connection forces within Emma. Louie the attachment, connection forces. In a more integrated person this would be experienced as being torn, being in conflict about whether to love/trust or not. Eve hated me with a purity that was stunning. Louie pretty much loved me, also a powerful experience.

In many ways Eve was my Waterloo. I never did figure out how to work with her. She seemed to shrink in her influence as time went on and as I continued to work with those who wanted to work with me. Even now, decades later, it bothers me that I couldn't figure out a way to connect with her. It feels like a deficit in my equipment as a therapist.

Eve tried to intimidate me, frighten me away. She did not succeed; the connection with Emma held. But she did succeed in preventing any meaningful exchange about that aspect of Emma's suffering and loss, which Eve embodied.

When I think of Eve, I am reminded now of the girl in junior high school who also had threatened me and said she would beat me up after school because I…? What did I do? I looked at her? Some hazy image from the girl's bathroom at school floats up, but really I don't remember doing anything except maybe staring at her. It was late in the 1950s or thereabouts. Today she also would have been covered in menacing tattoos.

The girl, Linda-something, did not follow through, but even more than 50 years later when I see her name in a reunion newsletter, I quake. I am *unable to* imagine her adult self, a regular citizen, married with grown children, evidently functional, *not* a criminal. For me she was still that chin-thrusting-out scary, pugnacious, tough as nails teenager: i.e. Eve.

I can now I see that the real bully in my life, the one I was most afraid of, was my father. It was he who overpowered me, although I resisted with all my teenage might. My father had a loud, fierce voice. When angry he had a tone, a frequency that could still evoke fear in me as an adult. "Don't argue with me!" he repeated to his argumentative, opinionated teenager, and even to his adult daughter. It was he who actually landed the psychic blows, not Linda.

Fear lives.

As I worked on this chapter I took a break. I took a walk. I was walking along listening to my audio book. There was mental chatter in the background: my own inner voice speaking disapprovingly, disparagingly and discouragingly about what I had just written: "You'll never figure this out. Who is going to want to read this? This isn't going anywhere. What made you think you could do this, you can't remember any details." And on and on.

Suddenly I realized I was listening to the legacy of my father's voice, now memorialized within me, one of my many inner voices. When I realized this was happening, I was able to forage about and find a more encouraging voice, one acquired in adulthood, bestowed on me by former therapists and benign influences in my adult life. I also remembered the encouragement of my writing group, the writing teacher and faithful colleagues, all who had expressed confidence in me.

I wondered about Eve and about my own inner demons. Emma felt Eve as alien, a demonic presence that she understood was part of her, but was not *felt* as part of her. She saw Eve as an enemy and did not feel as if Eve belonged to her. In contrast, I know the condemning voices are mine, and in time, I can even figure out where they come from, but I can't always control how deeply they affect me…just as Emma cannot control Eve.

After I caught myself talking trash to myself, I felt blocked. I didn't write for days. I considered giving up trying to write about Emma.

I ponder Nan and Eve again now, why they present as twins. I too have a timid, fearful, bullied ego state or part; maybe I have a bit of the bully in me as well. I can be sharp, inpatient, sarcastic, judgmental and aloof, I am told. Of this part I am barely aware most of the time and would *love* to disown it, not unlike a leprous limb. I was taken aback when a friend shared with me that she found herself worrying about a dent and dirt on her car when she came to pick me up, concerned that I would make some sharp comment. I was horrified that she would imagine that, not having noticed or cared about the appearance of her car, only grateful that she was giving me a ride.

Every bullied soul nourishes an inner bully who has been absorbed into their own personality as bully-ish qualities. That is just the ordinary fruit of trauma. In this, I am no different from Emma.

Now I think I understand why they are twins.

chapter 7
sabotage

"The concept of a single, unitary 'self' is as misleading as the concept of a single unitary 'brain.' The left and right hemispheres process information in their own unique fashion and represent a conscious left brain self- system and an unconscious right brain self-system."
— Allan Schore (prominent neuropsychologist, in Psychoanalytic Dialogues, 21, 2011.)

Many theorists of personality development believe that the notion of a unitary self is illusory. Evidence exists that in the beginning there are just states of being: "Now I am happy; now I am enraged; now I am hungry." The integrated, more or less unified self is a developmental accomplishment, not an original state. Trauma may interrupt that integration. The alternative view is that we are born whole and trauma shatters us. The longer I practice, the more I incline to the former view, that the mind is essentially "multiple" and knits together over time with a "good enough" environment. Integration as well as flexibility between states seems to afford us the best functioning.

I think of my grandson, who is such a sweetie when his baby sister is back at home and he gets to visit with his delighted grandparents as the sole object of their adoration. My mop-headed little Ollie is the perfect four-year-old gentleman: articulate, happy, even-tempered. He glows.

Ten minutes later, his mother arrives, baby sister in tow, and they have to leave. His composure melts; he is adamant, angry, aflame. He thrusts his face into hers, demanding recognition: "MOM!" He cannot be soothed.

These are two very distinct ego states. Ollie will eventually knit them together. But children experiencing trauma will not.

The Pixar movie *Inside Out* is an animated demonstration of the notion of multiple self-states. As the nine-year-old main character grows, she successfully integrates new self-states called "Joy" and "Sadness" to make a more mature and resilient, a larger self.

When there are multiple separated identities as there were in Emma, either this unification has been aborted because of extreme trauma, or it has been shattered by that trauma. Maybe both processes are at work. Maybe "self" is both multiple and unitary. The net effect with trauma is that numerous self-states are created and exist more or less cut off from other self-states. This is done in the service of survival. For instance, in Emma's case there were part-selves who hated the mother who failed to protect them and maybe had joined in the abuse, and there were those parts who denied her complicity; they loved and honored their mother throughout her very long life. The ability to construct a barrier between these contradictory, polarized feelings meant that Emma could obtain some nurturance, some tenuous attachment to the less abusive parent. She could feel love and be loved. As a result, she was able to love her children and later, her lover. I believe she came to love me (and I her).

Emma's part selves gradually made themselves known to me. They would either announce their presence when there was a switch from Emma, or I learned to discern over time the very subtle shifts in facial tone, vocal timbre, the way they held their bodies. The youngest child parts often sat on the floor.

All the "identities" were children, whether they admitted it or not. Some were exceedingly grandiose—Louie most of all—believing they held the key to all the secrets, that they were stronger, smarter and more powerful than anyone else. Similarly, my aforementioned grandson is convinced that he just needs a cape and a "magic" hat (ordered from Amazon) and he can extract a rabbit. He thinks he can teach the swimming teacher how to swim (his mother held to the same belief as a child). He doesn't need to go to a gymnastics class; he knows all the "tricks."

Grandiosity comes naturally to children. If all goes well, with time we grow more humble. But this is not true for Emma or those like her. Grandiosity comes with the trauma territory; it is fundamental to the process of creating parts. The illusion of amplified powers protects the helpless, totally overwhelmed child and allows her to stay alive. Perhaps the most inflexible belief of someone with DID is that they really need no one but themselves...their many, many selves. They can slice and dice their identities so they need only turn to one of their own parts to manage whatever is happening. When there is no one else safe to turn to, as was true in Emma's world, you must turn to yourself and yourself alone. While no conscious decision is made about this, it is an underlying principle in the creation of parts.

There are some obvious problems with grandiosity. No matter how smart and strong, no child can meet their own needs. And grandiosity is contagious. Therapists catch it from their patients. Without any real experience with multiplicity, I audaciously imagined I could do this by myself—I could learn and read and together, Emma and I could integrate all her parts.

Working with Emma initially enhanced my self-esteem. I felt I truly understood how dissociation worked when so many others didn't. I was working, learning and training in a sub-specialty that wasn't widely practiced, at least in my immediate geographic area at that time. Empowered by the work as I forged alliances with several of the part selves, it seemed to me that establishing communication between the selves would be pretty straightforward. I believed I would not be manipulated or stymied as so many others reportedly were. "I've got this," I silently bragged to myself. I am embarrassed to remember all this folly, my grandiosity.

The thing about grandiosity, though, is that eventually it shatters. It shattered both in Emma and in me.

Treating Emma was an empowering, almost an intoxicating experience initially and sporadically throughout the couple of decades of our work together. I had had my share of experiencing being overpowered and feeling helpless in my own home growing up. My parents believed in the supremacy of authority—"You need to respect your parents!"— and were unacquainted with the notion that empathy and warmth are as important as discipline.

My father especially was harsh, self-centered and distant. He inspired fear in me, and often, a sense of helplessness. One epithet echoes in my memory: "You idiot!" or *idiota* in Spanish. Looking back now through the lens of *his* trauma history, I can see that the fear and helplessness that he experienced repeatedly during his childhood during the Russian revolution—all "forgotten"—found its expression in his children, at least in me.

Overpowering others tends to conceal the actor's feelings of victimization. My father's voice, when he raised it, sounded like thunder and violence to me—echoes of his own childhood, no doubt. This is how I came to understand his cold and scary behavior toward his children.

Like my father's buried memories, Emma's parts were deeply invested in separateness. Louie would say with utter conviction, "Benji's memories are terrible. The kid should be euthanized." Louie disowned Benji's memories, they were not his!

The ego states initially build walls between themselves for very sound reasons: to preserve attachment to loved ones who were also perpetrators, to keep themselves from being overcome by memories that might stun them and crowd out the ordinariness and even the pleasures of everyday life, as well as to contain pain and suffering. Although Emma often "heard" Louie inside, she did not have access to other ego states who held even more ghastly memories than Louie did. If parts of Emma had not denied that the mother participated in some of the abuse, her attachment to the mother would not have held; she needed to love her mother and feel that she was as powerless as Emma was, a co-victim, not a perpetrator.

Dissociation also made it possible to learn, the chief developmental task of childhood. Emma had to have a part who could learn, and she created one! It was Missy who completed college and was able to become a talented and skilled professional, because Emma was able to create a part that held none of the terrible childhood memories. The "logic" of the system of partitioned selves was to keep the parts that needed to function from knowing the depths of torment they had suffered as children.

I worked primarily with Louie for many years. Louie evolved from a mischievous, almost hyperactive little kid to a balky, challenging teenager and eventually to an adult who managed "system Emma" and their lives. I almost always knew when Louie was there; he was a bit rougher than any of the girls and held himself more like a boy than like a woman. He even walked differently than Emma! As a teen, he strode about like the swaggering athletes I remember prowling the halls in high school. He seemed more sure of himself than some of the others. And there *were* others, but they came forward only reluctantly and briefly in the first phase of treatment.

In retrospect, I realize what a colossal mistake it was to allow such uneven access to the treatment. Louie was viewed by the system (of selves) as my favorite child, and they told me this on several occasions. "Louie is the son you never had." Maybe this was true. My privileging of Louie meant that I did not challenge his grandiosity; I felt that he could manage the treatment best and it was not necessary for me to have access to the whole system.

Overall, Louie seemed to have two jobs in the therapy. He was fiercely attached to me and thus kept all of Emma connected to the treatment. This was an essential ingredient for progress. He also protected "system Emma" from getting overwhelmed by keeping the worst memories—and therefore the youngest, most traumatized parts—away from the treatment. The latter suppressive function made work with Emma difficult, arduous and sometimes impossible. In retrospect, "system Emma" may have been waiting for me to mature as a therapist. I was much more sure of myself a decade or so into the treatment than I was at the outset, and got manipulated less often by Louie.

Emma's treatment proceeded in fits and starts. She would work for awhile and then decide that she (they) had to leave. In each instance, her departure seemed premature and abrupt and somewhat mystifying. Sometimes I felt quite frustrated and angry. My grandiosity was hard to hold onto at these junctures.

One particularly dramatic departure happened when I was forced to leave my home office. I was working there with Emma one day when a knock on the inner door, the door leading to my house, interrupted us. In all the years I had worked at home, neither of my children had ever knocked and disturbed a session. They were well trained. "It must be an emergency," I thought.

It was my youngest daughter: "There is a man at the front door of the house insisting that you come upstairs to talk to him. I told him you were working. He insisted."

I went to the door. A town official explained: "Someone has anonymously reported that you have an illegal office in your home." He showed me a postcard with a shaky scrawl and two misspelled sentences: "ofis in huse? Peeple go in and out?" I thought the writing was childish or infirm. In any event, it did me in. Our neighborhood was not zoned for any commercial use. The inspector wanted to inspect. I declined. I'd seen enough police dramas to know that he couldn't come in without my permission. *Wow. Shaken.* I had worked in the house, in a separate suite, for at least 15 years at that point. My neighbors had never objected.

I don't remember what I said or how I explained the interruption to Emma and later Louie when he emerged. Probably I just told them both the truth of what had happened.

I knew I didn't have to confirm the suspicions of the town inspector who seemed reluctant to press the matter anyway, but I decided it was probably best to rent an office in town and move my practice. I strongly suspected an elderly and cranky neighbor. I was going to confront her, but then she died.

Louie was now 15. I swear it seemed he had broader shoulders when he switched from Emma! He had integrated into himself a couple of angrier, sadistic, almost anarchic self-states and as a result had matured. This is the direction one wants to go in the treatment of DID—integration—but Louie was now a lot more difficult to get along with, as 15-year-olds often are.

Louie had always maintained that the birth parents were not his parents. He had essentially birthed himself; he just arrived one day when Emma could not endure what she had to endure. "I always knew they weren't my parents."

Sometimes you don't feel your hunger after a long fast until you have had a bite or two of food. As Louie grew older, he raged at me for what he felt had been a trick: by witnessing, empathizing, caring about and accepting him, I had excited the ravenous hunger for a *real* parent. He felt I had betrayed him. I was *only* a therapist who had other clients. The price of his maturity was an awareness of who I really was. He was giving me a very hard time at this point in the treatment. "Why should I listen to you? You don't really care. I pay you!" I learned much later that it was seeing other clients in my waiting room that triggered Louie's feelings of betrayal.

I found a "poem" that Louie had written at age 10—earlier in the treatment

> *I scream.*
> *I scream loud!*
> *Is this the reason no one likes me?*
> *I scream with hate, anger, and love*
> *Sometimes all mixed up*
> *But I just scream to let my feelings out.*
> *But today I scream because I am afraid to lose the new mommy.*
> *The one I love the most.*

Although I suspected that all my clients would be upset by the move to commercial space, in reality after one visit most settled into the new space and continued their work. Louie, on the other hand, *hated* my new office. There was traffic, parking was more difficult. It was larger, less "cave-like" than my basement office at home which seemed safer to him. Emma, the adult, was pretty mute on all of this. Louie's feelings seemed to drown out all else.

"This place even smells different. Your home office didn't always smell good, but it was home. There are too many people around, it isn't private!"

I suspected that this busy commercial building downtown was scary for all the children within Emma. "I grew up in that [home] office; you are evicting me!"

Louie came up with a solution. My other patients could go downtown to the new office, while he would remain seeing me in the home office. No one would notice. I did try this, but after a brief transitional period it became clear this was not manageable for me and he needed to come with me to the other office. Although I felt the need to make allowances for Louie given his world view, he had "grown up" in my office, I did not give in. I don't believe I was very articulate as to why; I just knew I couldn't. Weirdly, when I said, "Maybe I can't explain it, it just feels wrong," he calmly accepted this.

Louie now experienced me as colder, more formal, less engaged with him. "You are not my mother, you aren't any kind of mother!" This realization was devastating. Between rages, all he experienced was sadness and loss. He punished me with missed appointments, arriving ever later for the appointments that he did keep. This was all new. Previously, Emma and her cohort had almost *never* missed or cancelled and she was rarely late.

There was more self-injury happening than injury to me: Louie was gambling recklessly and losing more money than Emma and her partner could afford. Unexplained bruises and wounds on Emma's body were escalating. My grandiosity crumbled. As impressive and competent and smart as I felt at the outset to manage this complex system of identities, I was in equal measure diminished as the treatment seemed to be spinning out of control. Emma, the adult, was as bewildered as I; she had no idea what was going on. "I know we aren't getting anywhere," she said. "I can't seem to control what is happening." After many months, she left treatment. I was both relieved and disappointed. I had poured a lot of energy into trying to help Emma, but these several months in the new office were very frustrating and the case was feeling unmanageable.

Time passed, months. Finally Emma called asking to return to therapy. During our hiatus, she had made a serious suicide attempt. Having survived it, somehow everything had calmed down. There was no more fighting in the sessions, no more gambling, no more acting out. Emma said, "It was bad, the attempt, I took a lot of pills. I could have died. But I didn't. I think I was meant to live and to continue to work on myself."

Louie was older, wiser. But there also was no joy in Mudville: Louie was depressed.

It was Christmas, always a dark time for Louie. He began to speak of how he had participated in evil in the years of the active abuse and would always feel guilty about acts that he was either coerced into or convinced to perform. He did not tell me what these were, as he was deeply ashamed.

It is not unusual for the most sadistic and manipulative of perpetrators to put their victims in positions where they cannot escape performing acts that they will rue the rest of their lives. In the movie *Sophie's Choice*, a woman who had been interred in the Nazi death camp Auschwitz reveals to her lover after the war that she was forced by the guards to choose between her two children: which child would be gassed, which would survive. If she refused to choose, both children would die. This no-choice choice would haunt her forever. In the end, Sophie commits suicide. In the years of Emma's childhood, Louie and other parts of Emma had been put in similar positions by her parents more than once, and always as a young, bewildered child.

One day, I took a different tack: I wondered aloud, "Do you feel that you have hurt *me*, caused *me* harm?" There was some rapid switching between Louie and Emma; I could see it. Louie's more youthful voice became Emma's measured adult voice. There was a look of shock on Emma's face as Louie disappeared. Suddenly she knew. Louie "telegraphed" the news, letting Emma know what had been done.

It had now been almost two years since the enforced move out of my home office. I don't know why this question came to me at that moment. I had not thought about this previously. Instantly, both Emma and I put two and two together. Louie came clean, first through Emma and then as himself, and he was terribly ashamed. It was he who had written the postcard sent to the town officials. By doing so, he had attempted to hold onto the belief that he had become my son by exiling other patients to my commercial office. He would remain "home" with me. Emma said, "I didn't know. Oh, this is horrible!"

Later I realized that there was another layer to the caper: an attempt to sever the relationship. If Emma/Louie hurt me and I found out, I would get rid of him and he would no longer be attached to me and thus at risk for heartbreak. Eve, the twin who hated me, seemed to have gotten the upper hand and was a collaborator in this scheme and its sequelae. The suicide attempt was inspired by Louie's guilt over what he felt he had done to me and no doubt, further back as a young child, what hurt he had caused others in the context of his own torture and torment. Louie or someone else hinted darkly, "Eve wanted to do something much worse. We didn't let her." I never did learn what that was. I didn't press the issue. I think I didn't really want to know.

Louie told me a dream that very clearly spelled out the terrible emotional dilemma that he wrestled with.

> *I [Louie] am on a respirator. I can't figure out why I can't breathe. An x-ray reveals a carrot is stuck in my throat. I can't get it out. Eve [the twin] keeps turning off the respirator telling me I can breathe on my own. Eve insists I don't need*

an 'artificial partner.' When the respirator goes off I stop breathing. I try to turn it back on. This is hard to do because I can't breathe!

This is Emma/Louie/everybody's awful dilemma. It's an existential dilemma. We know instinctively that we need attachments to other humans to breathe, to live. But to be attached is to risk emotional pain. For Emma/Louie to be attached, to trust, was to risk death. She had been told repeatedly as a child not to trust anyone outside of a tight circle of family and her father's sinister friends who abused her.

The philosopher Schopenhauer described the existential challenge of all human intimacy: the porcupine's dilemma. Porcupines may huddle together to stay warm in cold weather. If they get too close, they hurt each other with their very sharp quills/spines. If they stay isolated, they risk freezing to death. In Emma/Louie's case, the spines were poisonous.

Louie's dream is such a vivid sketch of the porcupine's dilemma, with a more potent metaphor. A powerful part of Emma's system believed that they could "breathe on their own." This is the myth of self-sufficiency, the ultimate grandiosity. Turning me in to the town officials for an illegal office served two opposing goals: to get me all to themselves and to get rid of me. Those parts of the system that wanted me attached sought to get rid of my other patients. The parts that wanted me gone hoped I would dump them when I learned the truth of their misdeed. The latter forces felt that "an artificial respirator" was worthless. They could do without me, they always had, why risk everything now?

In the end, the desire and need for attachment won out. Emma returned to treatment, she re-engaged with me and Louie grew into an adult. And I didn't dump her.

Louie was hazy on the details, but what I came to understand was that "Eve," the dark twin, was able to influence him, or merge with him, because he was so unhappy when he recognized that I had other clients. "Growing up" had thrust Louie into the reality of who I truly was. Louie said it was Eve who hatched the plan about "busting" me and reporting me to the town officials. This was Louie disowning his own aggression, his own anger with me for having "duped" him into regarding me as a true mother, only to be unmasked as merely a therapist. Here is the artistry of dissociation at work; if you have a part in charge of anger and destruction, you can walk away from the consequences of your rage. This is not unlike the way a much younger child will blame an imaginary friend for having crayoned the walls, fully believing that she herself is blameless. The fact that Louie did not fully do this, that he actually felt horribly guilty about having participated in this event and confessed it to me, indicated greater integration, a signpost on the way to maturity.

In the end, without any direct assistance from me, the attachment forces triumphed and Louie returned to the therapy: repentant, wounded, but also older, wiser and ready to work again. He was in his early 20s, younger than Emma, but an adult. The teenager—argumentative, provocative and cantankerous—was gone.

This is not the first time I tell this story. Inevitably there is the question as to why I didn't end the therapy when the truth came to light. "How can you conduct a treatment when the client can put you at such risk?" my colleagues asked. "Weren't you afraid she would try to harm you again?"

I suppose here is where *my* grandiosity came back into play, as well as my very real attachment and affection for Emma and all her parts. The fact is, the displacement to my downtown office was not harmful to me. My professional life continued, flourished actually. My oldest child had left for college and I was enjoying a new freedom in my professional and personal life. It was kind of fun to get into my car and go to a downtown office like everybody else, not just down the stairs to my home office. I enjoyed being out and about in the commercial end of town, near shops and restaurants. I was freer of family responsibilities at that point and having an office downtown represented that newfound freedom.

Not suffering harm was a big part of my ability to reconcile with Emma. Additionally, I felt great relief to be working productively with her again. In the end, the majority of her partitioned selves chose attachment, voted for love. I didn't sense that danger lurked around the next corner. And in truth, it didn't. We continued, fruitfully, for many more years after this incident.

My confidence in Emma and in the whole system was probably as potent a healing factor as any well-thought out intervention on my part. I wasn't angry, so I didn't have to pretend that I wasn't angry. I had no impulse to retaliate, so I didn't need to suppress that impulse either. And Louie grew from this; he actually got older. He was now in his 20s, close to the adult Emma's age at that point.

Managing the complexities of a system like Emma's is a great challenge to any clinician, and I have had my share of failures with others like her along the way. This therapy could have ended differently. The bullying twin Eve could have triumphed. Emma could have been successful in her suicide attempt. And even after surviving, Emma could have hidden her shame and not returned to treatment. Resilience is a mystery to me. Why does one fractured soul survive and another not? Why does one with so many secrets come to therapy and another not? Why did Emma stick it out when so many others are not able to?

Many questions. No answers.

chapter 8
missy

When Emma was a young teen, her older brother Mitch—whom she adored and idealized—precipitously ran away from home, away from the father who had brutalized and pimped them both. The father's alcoholism had progressed and he had become even more dangerous to the family than before. Emma was devastated. She had always perceived the mother as favoring and protecting Mitch. She remembered being left alone with the father when it looked like he might actually murder Mitch. Emma's mother ran off with her son and did not return for several days. "I thought she was gone for good. I was terrified." This was not the only time that her mother abandoned her, but for Emma, it was the worst time.

Emma was stunned that her brother would leave her. With Mitch at home, although there was no real safety, at least had a companion in terror. Perceiving more danger in his absence, Emma decided to make her get-away as well.

It seems somewhat miraculous that Emma was able to negotiate an exit with a foster family of her choice. A teacher at school had picked up enough clues from her behaviors and whatever bruises and scars were visible to understand that she was being abused. Emma did not provide many details to him, only enough confirmation for him to proceed; there may have been some part-self that stepped up and broke the seal of secrecy enough to let the teacher into some hints of what she was enduring.

The teacher notified protective services and they came to investigate the family. This alarmed the parents and before the investigation could go further, the mother agreed to let Emma be placed.

Emma was both relieved and wounded by her mother's decision. Some child ego states recognized that the mother was granting her a reprieve from the unrelenting abuse of the father, while some felt that she was being sacrificed: the mother chose her relationship to the father over her.

The foster family proved to be safe but not a loving haven for the latter years of Emma's adolescence. There was intense rivalry with the other siblings and the mother of the family had never really signed onto the rescue. She was cold and sometimes rejecting of Emma.

Missy emerged as a new ego state during this period. She was created to function well in this new environment and she did just that. She had no trauma memories, was competent and able to concentrate and manage school. She endured as a major player even after Emma left the foster family. When I came on the scene, Missy became my co-therapist, helping me to navigate the choppy waters of Emma's system.

Missy was particularly helpful with Louie, who—much like any behavior-disordered 10 year old boy—frequently veered close to a perilous edge. When I met Louie, Emma was about to lose her license for speeding and moving violations; Louie had too often been at the wheel. Emma was terribly upset that she could not control these behaviors. Missy and I worked together to rein in Louie's more extreme behavior and she helped me begin to build co-operative ties within Emma. For Louie, Missy was an internal wise and caring parental figure. Missy identified for me the other ego states that were known at that time, what they were about and their relationship to each other. She and Angel both were my allies in the initial phase of therapy and they were easier to get along with than some of the others.

More importantly, Missy was a trusted guide for Emma and her parts. She ordered books for Emma and the younger ones also that explained DID to them in a reassuring and age-appropriate way. Missy was comforter and mother. Like Angel, Missy was reliably present for all the inner children. She was calm and wise. But unlike Angel, she functioned in the outside world as well as within Emma and could come forward when she was needed.

Missy decided in the early phase of treatment that she needed to integrate and merge with Emma. She had decided this was best for the overall system. If she integrated, the system would be stronger and the younger parts would turn to me rather than to her for help. Integration is not unlike the natural process of maturation that takes place for all of us as we grow. Within Emma, clearly this process had been distorted, disjointed and atypical. I did not resist Missy's decision to integrate with Emma, to cease to exist as separate, to join and strengthen Emma, but I did regret it, because she could no longer advise me on navigating through the labyrinthine world of Emma and her mates.

Missy's decision to integrate, unprompted by me, meant that "the greater Emma," now felt safe enough to rely on my guidance. But I did not rejoice. I felt more alone after she ceased to be separate.

It must have been December, for on this day Emma was talking about celebrating Hanukah with her Jewish foster family and she could not remember the name of the candelabra that they lit at that time of year. But this was *the* day, the day we were preparing for the merging of two separate ego states, Emma and Missy. Missy explained the need for this change: "I will miss Louie and the others," she noted sadly. "It's really especially hard to leave him. But I have left him my room [inside], so he will feel safe. You know, I was created to do this, to hold a reservoir of strength so that when the time came, I could give it back to Emma. Now is the time. Now that you are here, May."

Louic and some of the others were both angry with me and frightened of what life would be like without Missy, without a distinct ego state on

whom they could rely for guidance, for wisdom. She has been there for so
long. "What will I do without her?" wailed Louie. Transferring some of
that dependence onto me felt risky for him and the other self-states. They
now had to bring to *another person*, not just another part of themselves,
their pain and worries, and most importantly their memories. This in and
of itself was a heroic leap of faith, given the relentless betrayals they had
suffered. This pattern of fury and fear continued into the future when
other integrations took place, with or without my assistance.

Missy explained: "What the children don't understand is that this is
not a death, even though I will not feel myself as separate and neither
will they."

I was deeply moved by the altruism of Missy volunteering to
integrate with the "greater Emma" to give up her separateness in the
interests of the greater good, strengthening the system as a whole.
Unlike virtually all of the other ego states, she did not defend to the
death, as they do and did thereafter, their own separateness. They were
all mostly like Pinocchio, who wants to be really, real: a real boy, not a
puppet. I felt deep in my muscles an ache, a body marker for both their
grief and my own. I was so sorry to lose Missy, my able co-therapist.
What would *I* do without her wisdom, her guidance? I cannot hide my
tears. The genius of a system that holds onto and sequesters a "reservoir
of strength" only to return it to its source at the right time is profoundly
moving to me. "It is good to see that you are human," Missy says to me
kindly, as she notices the dampness on my face.

Later in the treatment, any integrations that took place happened
spontaneously, without my assistance, but at this point, I was learning
how to do this work and implemented an imagery technique that I had
read about. "And now we begin." I suggested to the adult Emma and
to Missy the following:

"You two are like two concentric circles that can now move into
one larger, stronger circular structure. You will be more resilient in that
form." Emma, like other individuals whose personalities are structured
similarly, could easily induce a trance-like state in herself, and given that

most ego states were on board with Missy's plan, upset but basically on board, it was easily accomplished.

> *Emma, Missy, visualize the circle that represents each of your identities, your selves; see the circles as separate but slowly moving toward each other. Slowly they move, getting closer and closer until they overlap. Now they overlap more, and as they keep moving eventually they become one. When the circles have completely joined, they have become one larger, stronger, more beautiful circle than when separate. Take your time. When you are ready open your eyes.*

What I saw was something like a speeded up time-lapse video, an individual maturing before my eyes. Emma's face softened ever so slightly; there was a shift in how she held her body. A new, a different Emma looked around the office taking in the scene as if she had never seen it before, and indeed she hadn't. Her eyes were now new. Literally.

I knew that there was someone different in the room now, different from the woman who entered my office many minutes ago. The resonance, the vibration between us had a different pitch, a different quality. Emma, now merged with Missy, took back what had always been hers. She was more womanly, more relaxed, more present. Slowly she settled into herself.

"I can't see with these," said Emma. She removed her glasses and looked around my smallish cozy basement office. She looked down at the beige upholstered, only slightly stained couch of modern Scandinavian design, then looked across at me, maybe six or seven feet away, as I perched upon my rocking chair. There was wonder in her eyes, newborn wonder. She held her body slightly more upright, slightly more relaxed as she looked around. If a posture can be more settled, more grounded, then that was the new Emma's posture. There was more substance to the less-androgynous woman now before me.

She glanced to the left at the door: "That's the door to my home," I explain. And then several feet in front of her: *"That's the door to the outside, the waiting room, bathroom and the yard."*

The art on the walls had stayed the same for many, many years. I had posters of a Hockney drawing ("Seated Woman") and a photo of Cartier-Bresson, both purchased at the Tel Aviv Museum. In later years, child ego states would insist that the seated woman in the Hockney drawing, a woman with blondish hair, was a picture of Sydney, a woman they had known was my friend and their group therapist for a few years. They also knew that she had died and in retrospect, I think this may have been meant to soothe me, imagining that her picture was right there in my office. My navy pin dot rug was one that Emma had spent years crawling around on as child ego states each took "a turn upon the stage." Emma looked as if she had never seen any part of this room before.

Still trying to focus her "new" eyes, the new Emma said, "One pupil seems to be larger than the other. I really can't see out of these glasses. I feel like I've just gained 35 pounds or so. My clothes feel so tight they hurt! My head feels kind of heavy." We both laughed when she added, "I have an urge to go shopping and I *hate* to shop! Ha! I want to have my ears pierced, of all things."

Emma, short and slight, always dressed in simple t-shirts, sweatshirts and jeans was often mistaken for a young boy. Missy was less boyish than Emma and more stereotypically female, unlike the many child ego states I came to know. Emma was now sensing the "Missy influence."

"You look different and feel different to me" she said, "Less distant." Missy trusted me more than many of the other ego states.

When the session ended, I escorted Emma down the long macadam driveway from my office to the street where her car was parked. Emma was a bit shaky, disoriented, squinting. She would get new glasses after this. She told me later that the bank required her to sign new signature cards as her handwriting had changed as well. "The whole world looks different," she said as we walked. She was happier, delighted with herself as she felt smarter. And suddenly: "I can remember the name of the candelabra for Hanukah, a menorah!" Missy, unlike Emma, identified as Jewish, as she had first joined the system while living with the Jewish foster family.

When I finally left New Jersey, moved to DC and ended our 20-year treatment, Emma and I exchanged music mixes to mark our time together. Each ego state had made their own selection, each song signifying something important of their experience of themselves. My mix was simpler, just songs that I liked, but looking back on the list I see a song I had selected by Dar Williams that could well have been Missy's anthem, Missy's heart, Missy's purpose. I chose it from a mix that I had made for my youngest daughter before she gave birth to her first child. It was the last song on the list and signified to me the poignancy of letting go of our offspring as they grow into themselves. I think Missy, as the good mother of "system Emma," felt this about the child ego states she had looked after. Missy was everything that the biological mother was not, everything they wished she had been. And it's all in this song.

A few stanzas of "The One Who Knows":

Time it was I had a dream
And you're that dream come true
An' if I had the world to give
I'd give it all to you

I'll take you to the mountains
I will take you to the sea
I'll show you how this life became
A miracle to me

You'll fly away but take my hand until that day
So when they ask how far love goes
When my job's done you'll be the one who knows

All the things you treasure most
Will be the hardest won
I will watch you struggle long
Before the answers come

But I won't make it harder
I'll be there to cheer you on
I'll shine the light that guides you down
The road you're walking on

You'll fly away but take my hand until that day
So when they ask how far love goes
When my job's done, you'll be the one who knows

chapter 9
joey, magic and monarchs

A few minutes after I hung up the phone with my daughter, I remembered Joey's prophecy. It was toward the end of our work together when he knew I would be moving to be near children and grandchildren, too far away to be able to continue the treatment. For some reason, Joey was sitting on the floor, I was on the couch; not our usual positions. Perhaps there had been a switch from a much younger child part. Joey was now at least a teen, maybe older. We were talking about the future: my future. He looked up at me: "You will have five grandchildren in all."

"No," I correct "four." My oldest daughter had two already and seemed to be finished, and the younger one had one but was planning another. He thought for a moment, seemed to be listening inside: "No, five," he insisted. And now, given the phone call, I had an inkling he might be right. Daughter #1 was pregnant with her third child. Joey had clairvoyant abilities and, this talent—and it couldn't be mind-reading for I had no inkling this was in the cards—was borne out. More recently, many years after the conversation, when Emma got in touch via email, Joey was not above crowing about the accuracy of his prediction: "Told ya you would have 5 grand kids! LOL."

Joey—the *real* boy, not the part of her—had been Emma's best friend, confidante, companion and consoler before she was six years old. His life experience was much like hers, in that he experienced severe abuse and terror at the hands of family and multiple abusers. Although both of these young children were warned not to speak of their shared experiences to each other, they did. And they did so on one of the darkest days of Emma's young life. They whispered to each other about the people who had abused them while playing ball near a busy street. The ball rolled out to the middle of the street, Joey ran after it and died instantly, hit by a speeding car. Emmie, the young ego state who held this awful story, was later to tell me, "I saw the light go out of his eyes." She watched him die.

At age six, the finality, the irreversibility of death is still a shaky concept. Emma was told by her parents not to speak of it. Joey's family soon moved away and she never saw them again. Emma dimly remembers the funeral and that her older brother was silly and fooled around in the church. She'd wished at the time that she could feel as light-hearted as he. Instead, she felt the full weight of the occasion, although she didn't quite understand what was going on.

Emmie and Joey remained bonded, Joey vividly remembered as he entered her inner world as a distinct ego state. He was still alive inside and deeply loved. One of the songs that Emmie chose for the going-away CD she made for me was "Coming Home" by Gavin Rossdale. The lyric of the song acknowledges the loss. She knows the real boy is no more. Here is part of the sad lyric:

> *Here I am without you*
> *Drink, to all that we have lost*
> *Mistakes we have made*

Everything will change
But, love remains the same

Find a place where we escape
Take you with me for a space

Another song was "Better in Time" by Leona Lewis:

It's been the longest winter without you
I didn't know where to turn to
See somehow I can't forget you
After all we've been through

Emma utilized the adaptive capacity of dissociation she already possessed at age six to preserve her lost beloved, deep within. The capacity of your average six-year-old to grieve is very limited. The finality of death may or may not have actually taken hold in a child so young, even a very bright child. Up until age seven, an ordinary child in an ordinary environment understands death as a *reversible* state. I've notice that my own grandchildren could be cavalier about death at age five, but filled with fear by age seven, when they understood more.

Emma was not ordinary, nor was her environment. Secrecy was imposed on all matters and as Joey was a fellow victim in Emma's world, there was no discussion after the accident of his life or his death. Left to cope on her own with no solace, no explanation, no support from either parent nor from the community of child abusers of which she and Joey were a part, her solution was to hold onto Joey. She made him a *real* part of her.

In some ways Emmie and Joey were another pair of twins, like Eve and Nan. Frozen into place at age six by tragedy, they continued to be there for each other, inside.

The prologue to *Orphan Train* by Christina Baker Kline describes a similar process, one perhaps more familiar to us. She writes:

I believe in ghosts. They're the ones who haunt us, the ones
who have left us behind. Many times I have felt them around

*me, observing, witnessing, when no one in the living world knew
or cared what happened.*

   *I am ninety-one years old and almost everyone who was once
in my life is now a ghost.*

   *Sometimes these spirits have been more real to me than people,
more real than God. They fill silence with their weight, dense
and warm, like bread dough rising under cloth. My gram, with
her kind eyes and talcum-dusted skin. My da, sober, laughing.
My mam, singing a tune…and they console and protect me in
death as they never did in life.*

Joey was that kind of ghost for Emma; dead but ever-present.

Louie was possessive of me and kept many of the other ego states
outside of the treatment, limiting their time and thus their relationship
with me. He craved whatever nurture was available to him in this setting
but he also felt the need to control the "action" and the system. It did
not feel safe to him to let others step forward with whatever memories
or fragments of memories they held. Therefore, although the ego
state Joey did show up in the early years of the treatment from time to
time, he was not front and center until much later. He would appear
occasionally to tattle on Louie, or to fill in a fact that Louie did not
know about. In one session as Louie worked through one of the most
devastating of his abuse memories, Joey darted in quite unexpectedly
and whispered, "She was there. Mom was there, she saw this happen."
The adult Emma did not usually see the mother as a collaborator to
the abuse, but evidently Emma's mother knew and she was a passive,
perhaps helpless witness.

Emma left treatment for a long stretch, several years, when Louie
decided that he and the others had done enough work. His back was
straight, he held my gaze when he insisted repeatedly "Some things
need to be taken to the grave." He was determined but sad too, that
he had to carry on alone. I knew that they were not finished but there
was no talking him out of this. Ruefully, at that point I had to file the
treatment in the "partial failure" file.

When Emma returned almost exactly three years later; she was at her wits end. Louie explained that for at least a year he had been struggling to deal with increasing fears of going outside. He had been staying inside to avoid triggers, scenes or people that would evoke flashbacks that he was desperate to keep at bay. Emma had divorced, recoupled with a well-to-do partner, a woman this time, and was no longer working outside the home, so being in the house all the time was feasible in theory, but unachievable in practice. The memory fragments kept coming. Louie had his own treatment plan for his anxiety which was to force himself to walk the dogs outside for at least an hour every day. Finally he had to admit that his plan did not stem the growing tide of anxiety that he was experiencing There was no getting away from the fragments of memories pressing in on him. He turned to me as a last resort.

Louie was different as an adult. Lou, as he was known now, had become very controlling and even more grandiose than at younger ages. Control was his credo: "The more I control everyone [inside] the smoother everything will go." But anxiety was building and he could no longer suppress all the younger folk within; he was discovering newer ones. This was scary, a whole new layer of ego states. Louie told me, "We didn't know they were there. We heard this whispering. It was Joey's fault, his meditating did it."

At this point, when therapists working with DID feel they have achieved a degree of stability and some integration of parts in collaboration with their patients, it can be disheartening to encounter a new layer previously unknown. Even though I had read about this phenomena many times and knew to interpret it as evidence of progress, i.e. there was enough trust established that Emma could go deeper and achieve more healing, it still felt like "back to the salt mines" at a more profound and difficult level. There were more, grimmer memories to be worked with. Joey was both a gateway to the deepest levels of suffering within Emma and to the younger and younger splits within "system Emma" that held her history.

When Joey finally showed up, he "outed" Emma's mother as not just a passive bystander to the abuse of her children, but an active participant. Louie had been the target of sexual abuse and about this vulnerability he was ashamed. For him it was worse than the violence he had experienced. It was not the image he had of himself or that he wanted to project. He was the "controller" not the victim. It was in these later stages of the treatment that I learned that Louie had kept Joey behind the scenes. It now appeared that Joey could be stifled no more.

When Emma's mother approached her sexually, it was to Lou that Emma automatically switched. More than likely, the mother was DID herself and there was a certain part that resonated with Lou and pulled him in. Joey uncovered this secret: "You should ask Louie about Mom. She did stuff to him."

Joey had a strong spiritual side. He meditated and went to conferences having to do with the paranormal. He seemed at first to want to cultivate and develop his spiritual side. He appeared to be clairvoyant. He had gotten Emma into a great deal of debt by employing his psychic abilities in Atlantic City, winning vast sums of money gambling and then quickly losing it all. "I knew how the cards would turn out," he explained. "But why did you lose so much money if you were guided?" I asked. "Well when I stopped hearing them [his spirit guides] I just kept guessing. That didn't turn out so well," he admitted, with some dismay. Later he told me that the spirit guides sensed a lot of "darkness, bad people" in the gambling rooms and he stopped going.

Yes, Joey had spirit guides. In a way it made sense—he was product of a sudden death, the boy Joey. He had a foot in both worlds. A sixth sense, some manifestation of psychic ability is not rare with people who have experienced severe trauma in childhood. It's almost as if the kind of vigilance that young victims have to develop to survive edges over into an extra sense that attunes them to another reality. At least that's one way of accounting for this phenomenon. I never questioned it. It served Joey well, it got him out of Atlantic City and it almost always aligned

with my own treatment goals and assessments. I believe it was the spirit
guides who told Joey that I was going to have five grandchildren.

Joey's spirit guides, or whatever they were, were not ego states or
part-selves. Like Angel, they did not have traumatic memories, or any
memories at all as far as I knew. They did not come out in the treatment
to talk and work with me. They were present only to Joey.

Another reason Emma was forced back into treatment was that
Joey's meditations had led to an "awakening" of yet younger splits
within Emma, parts we hadn't known about before. "I heard whispers
in the attic, young children," he reported. The attic was a metaphor for
a place inside, deeply buried within Emma's mind that Joey perceived
during his meditations. Everyone within Emma was stunned that they
existed. Each young ego state had a tale to tell. No one else, not Joey,
Louie, Emmie, Nan nor Missy had these memories. It seemed that Joey
brought them with him and they were to guide the next many years of
work together. It was Benji (whom we meet in the next chapter) who
would tell their stories.

The Joey expression of Emma was very appealing; he reminded me
of the younger Louie, with the same vitality, energy, restless curiosity
and enthusiasm for learning, the same determination to supplant all the
other ego states and dominate the entire system. Joey's innocence, his
cheerful optimism drew me in. I wondered if the Emma/Joey resembled
the boy Joey who had died so many years earlier.

Louie did not like my attentions to Joey and continued to try to
keep him out of the treatment. This was an ongoing struggle, but I was
now older and wiser, more seasoned as a therapist, and Louie could not
manipulate me as easily as he had earlier. I stuck with Joey and urged
Louie to work with him. Eventually he did. Joey became his aide-de-
camp, helping Louie shoulder the burdens that were now his; Louie
had assumed a lot of adult Emma's responsibilities.

Like the Russian Matryoshka—wooden dolls of decreasing size
nesting within one large wooden doll—many of the boys seemed to
be nested within one another and came forward only as the treatment

progressed. From Joey came Benji, from Benji came other younger parts, each holding a piece of the worst of the trauma memories.

Joey had a great love for the out of doors, hiking, fishing, boating and gardening. Gardening was of particular importance to Joey. When Joey took over for the adult Emma, he demonstrated a great proficiency in organic gardening techniques. His vegetables were robust and tasty. Joey also farmed marijuana, which he grew hydroponically indoors so as not to be discovered, an expensive and painstaking hobby that yielded very high quality weed. The pot was grown for home consumption. It was disturbing to hear that everyone in the family was an enthusiastic, almost daily consumer. The only one over whom I had any influence was Emma/Joey of course, but on this issue I had no influence on her either.

Of all the sub-personalities Joey was by far the most devoted pothead. What may have started as a hobby became heavy drug usage, functioning to bury psychic pain and blot out the memories, the images that were flooding in. The spirit guides chided Joey repeatedly about this, telling him that his pot usage was hurting him; weakening him and defeating the work we were trying to do in the therapy. Joey in turn did everything he could to block the messages from the spirit guides and from me.

Joey was being assaulted with Benji's memories, Benji being the Matryoshka doll within Joey. Benji's memories were the worst and Joey was being bombarded. I could not come up with the right interventions to help Joey with all of this, to help him titrate the intrusive memories. Always resourceful, he came up with his own solution: massive doses of weed. Eventually even this didn't work. The system at some level needed to accept Benji's memories as true and as something that had happened to all of them in the past, something that they had all survived. And they couldn't. "That boy just needs to go away!" insisted Louie and Joey, the major players within Emma who were repeatedly assaulted by flashbacks.

It was toward the end of the treatment, after more than 15 years of work, that a new solution presented itself. I was closing my office, ending with all of my clients in New Jersey and moving out of state. Without preamble, without warning, Joey did go away. The ego state Emmie, now fully adult, explained: "I had to let go of Joey. He was in too much pain. He couldn't deal with Benji's memories anymore. I have to accept that the boy Joey died in that car accident."

The system had achieved a partial integration. Joey had come from her after the car accident and went back to her. Emmie was now stronger and at least for a time, Joey was no more. Emmie, now united with Joey, could manage Benji and all of his memories. Joey could not.

Recently we gave one of our grandsons a "butterfly garden" which is a kit for growing caterpillars and butterflies. As we did so I remembered Joey's fascination with monarch butterflies. Joey became a monarch expert. He studied everything he could find on the internet. He found milkweed growing in their yard, an essential food for the right kind of caterpillar. He closely observed the formation of cocoons, took pictures, protected the chrysalis, sometimes removing them to a humid bathroom "so no predators would disturb them." He watched ever so carefully as they became brilliantly striped monarchs. "They fly from New Jersey to Mexico. Isn't that amazing?" He was so excited when he learned to distinguish male monarchs from females by subtle markings on their wings. Emma and her partner took many pictures and even gave me some cocoons to watch as they developed on my deck and magically transformed. It was fun, it was fascinating and it promoted Joey's growth.

I got very involved in this process with Joey and encouraged it. It seemed like a powerful if unconscious metaphor for the personal growth and transformation that was taking place within the cocoon of treatment. As with the butterflies, it was often mysterious what went on within the chrysalis of treatment. There was always uncertainty: the fog of treatment. Would a butterfly ever emerge? Would it survive predators? Would Emma make it all the way to Mexico?

chapter 10
benji

Ben, the two of us need look no more,
We both found what we were looking for.
With a friend to call my own,
I'll never be alone, and you, my friend, will see,
You've got a friend in me.

Ben, most people would turn you away;
I don't listen to a word they say.
They don't see you as I do;
I wish they would try to.
I'm sure they'd think again if they had a friend like Ben.
—Don Black, "Ben" as sung by Michael Jackson

As I mentioned earlier, Emma and I exchanged music "mixes" toward the end of our 20 year collaboration: music that we liked, songs that were meaningful to each of us, burned onto a couple of CDs. These would be mementos of our time together, and help us both manage an ending that felt like a heartbreaking abandonment to Emma and was painful and wrenching for me as well. Whose idea this was, I can't remember, but I was not comfortable with any other kind of gift. This was a great one, one I treasure many years later.

I was surprised when I finally received the mix to see that each of the "inner children" had chosen their own songs. Although Emma did not seem to be aware of this, many of their choices had meaning, spoke to who they were and where they hurt.

The song *Ben*, by Michael Jackson, was Benji's choice. It could be the anthem of all the part-selves, but I think it fit Benji the best. I will call him Benji, although that is not the name he called himself.

All of the "children" felt the profound isolation referred to in the song and their creative solution to this terrible problem was to create "friends," alternate ego states, that no one else knew was there. The memories that Benji held, however, may have inclined him to feel the most profound isolation. He was isolated from everyone on the outside, relationships that Emma had. And he was shunned by those inside as well.

> *Ben, you're always running here and there,*
> *You feel you're not wanted anywhere.*
> *If you ever look behind and don't like what you find*
> *There's something you should know, you've got a place to go.*
> *I used to say I and me, now it's us, now it's we.*
> *I used to say I and me, now it's us, now it's we.*

"Ben" is a simple ballad, the tempo slow, the undertone sad. A very young Michael Jackson sung it as if it were *his* anthem. The first time I met Benji, many years before we exchanged CD mixes, there was nothing slow or measured about him. The "sad" did not show. *His* tempo was feverish, chaotic, dissonant. He literally tore through my office, crawling on all fours. It took many years to see the "Ben" who was underneath that hectic pace.

While Louie had a swagger, an energy to him even when he was very young, Benji was more agitated, restless, energetic and frantic. On the day that Benji first appeared, there was a sudden unanticipated switch from Louie. What I understand this to mean is that Benji was "related" to Louie, a younger split, a representation of an ego state that contained the horrors that were too much for Louie. He was "thrown outside" by the system, maybe to test if it was time for his story to be told.

Usually Emma or Louie would recede in response to my request to let another ego state come forward, because one of the others could best tell the story that needed to be told that day. But on this day, there was no transition; suddenly there was a much younger ego state in the room. Emma's body shifted and as with all shifts, I felt it in my own body, in my racing pulse, on my skin. Louie was no longer there. Another boy part of Emma, and he was clearly a young boy, slipped to the floor and started moving around the office, scurrying, scuttling, flinging himself about in a distracted, unfocused fashion. He looked around, he clearly didn't recognize this place, but he didn't appear frightened; more curious, and exploring, roughly handling all the items that he could reach.

All the boy ego states were clearly boys; the way they held themselves, their boldness, their movements quick and heedless, so much like the toddler or little boy movements of my grandsons. Except my grandsons run around joyfully; Benji, not so much. Within Emma, boy ego states were *stereotypically* boys, sometimes almost caricatures of boys. They liked outdoor boys' activities like fishing and boating and running fast. The girls were caricatures as well. They were soft spoken, sometimes timid, stereotypically girlish. They liked reading and drawing, maybe even poetry. These states were representations of a young child and as such they were pretty unidimensional. Emma saw her older brother as stronger than she and less vulnerable to abuse. The boy ego states were based on the illusions of Emma's childhood —boys as stronger and less vulnerable to abuse—for in reality, her brother was no safer than she from the predators.

There was something very primitive about Benji when he first appeared. Most of Emma's parts seemed to have had some sense of appropriate boundaries. Benji had none. When a new ego state appeared, they were usually shy. Benji was not.

From my notes:

He is on the floor inspecting everything he sees, managing to make a toy out of an electrical outlet, the wooden feet of the couch, a pencil that has fallen on the floor. I have an oil-filled metal radiator in my office; it is off, not hot, and somehow Benji has converted it into a toy. He pushes the kneeling chair parked at my desk, spinning it. It's a rather worn and wobbly thing and I fear that he will break it if I don't stop him. My office is neither large nor cluttered but somehow he finds dozens of things to handle and endanger. He is grabbing papers off my desk, a stapler, pencil, pens, a clock; he snatches at some art glass paper weights that I dearly prize. Eyes darting around the room, not looking at me but at objects in the room, he is not responsive in the least to my increasingly desperate objections to his messing with my stuff. "Please don't…" And now I am darting around the room rescuing my stuff. He moves like a hyperactive three-year-old who has yet to learn boundaries and a sense of the other. Is he trying to tell me something? Why is he here so suddenly, without preamble or introduction? I have all sorts of questions and no answers. Anarchy.

> *Ben, you're always running here and there,*
> *You feel you're not wanted anywhere.*
> *If you ever look behind and don't like what you find*
> *There's something you should know, you've got a place to go.*
> *I used to say I and me, now it's us, now it's we.*
> *I used to say I and me, now it's us, now it's we.*

"Who are you?" I asked. "Do you know me?" No answer. "What is your name?"

"Benji."

"Have I met you before?"

"No".

"Do you know who I am?" No answer. He really did seem interested in me, only in my things, things I really don't want him to touch.

"Is there something you want to say to me?" Benji said nothing; he just kept scuttling around the room, grabbing things.

I bent low from my chair trying to catch his eye, trying to connect with him. No luck. Soon it was time to end the session.

If Benji had been a "real" little boy, not a grown woman in therapy, I might have been tempted to stop him physically, to hold him in a tight embrace. I would have been embodying the necessary boundary. But Benji was part of a grown woman and I did not have a contract with Emma to do this.

Not once in all the time I had worked with Emma had I ever had trouble ending a session, shifting back to an adult capable of walking out of my office more or less intact. There had been a tacit understanding that we could not do this kind of outpatient treatment without a capacity for transitioning back to a stable adult at the end of a session.

This was different. Benji did not seem to know his way back inside, as all the others had. I did not know if he was unable or unwilling to let the adult Emma return.

I called for some ego state with more executive function than this boy. "Louie, Emma, you need to come forward now, it's the end of the session."

This usually worked. Not that day. In retrospect I realize that Emma had never pushed me the way this young one did, beyond what I could comfortably handle.

I had a huge problem. I could not let Emma leave in this state. Benji could not drive home, Benji could not leave the office safely. I barred the door. My usual self-assurance, the therapist persona that manages to represent that she knows what she's doing, began to crack.

My stomach churns, my mouth dry, my anxiety is mounting, along with the volume of my voice. I am frantic. I have other patients coming in, someone will be in my waiting room soon, and will hear the ruckus. In the end I am almost yelling. I am ashamed that I have lost control of the situation.

Eventually Benji found his was back inside and Emma returned and left the office. He didn't come again for many years. He waited until I ripened, until I had a better grasp on how to deal with abject terror.

Ben, most people would turn you away;
I don't listen to a word they say.
They don't see you as I do;
I wish they would try to.
I'm sure they'd think again if they had a friend like Ben

Years later I would realize that what looked like anarchy was closer to panic. Benji did not know where he was or who I was, or whether he was safe with me. No one he had ever encountered, in his slice of Emma's life, had ever been safe. He assumed I was not safe either, and in that awful first encounter I proved him right by yelling at him! Furthermore, everyone within the system, all of Emma's inner children, rejected Benji, hated him. He was known as "bad," they all told me sometime later. I saw that he assumed this identity and initially behaved in ways that were very difficult for *me* to tolerate. Actually I couldn't tolerate it and didn't know what to do about it. The solution of Emma's system was to keep him inside and not challenge my vulnerability. After much experience with Emma's ego states I was a wee bit wiser and able to interpret his misbehavior as a manifestation of fear. This made all the difference. From that point on we could work together.

Years later we had a more productive interaction.

Benji appears suddenly in my office. Again sitting on the floor, looking vigilant, wary of me, ready to bolt…

Me: Who's here?

Benji: Me, Benji.

Me: Hi Benji. I'm so glad you came back.

B: You yelled at me

M: I did. I didn't understand. I didn't see how scared you were to be in my office. I'm really sorry. I didn't realize that you didn't know who I was or what I would do. I'm really, really sorry.

B: Oh, OK.

Benji never, ever gave me trouble again. He learned to trust me and confide in me the very worst of "system Emma's" memories. At this point "system Emma" and I had done a lot of work together and undoubtedly this helped Benji ease into a more collaborative mode. It wasn't just that I was a more seasoned therapist. But that did help.

With time, I came to understand how terribly sad Benji was as well as how convinced of his own depravity. He had not only witnessed a terrible atrocity but been made to feel complicit in it: Sophie's choice once again. He was trapped in an overwhelming memory, unable to update his reality and know that he was now free of his perpetrators and entirely innocent of the terrible crimes he had assumed were his. He felt literally trapped in a room where he had witnessed a murder.

Benji's world was a world of flashback. He lived, or lived before treatment, in constant flashback. I can only be vague about Benji's story, as I will not betray Emma's trust by going into too much detail. I will only say that Benji had witnessed the abuse and murder of another child and was then manipulated into believing that he had been responsible for the crime. He had carried the weight of this knowledge, of this guilt and terror, for the whole system. No one in system Emma knew of these memories. Benji was walled off from the rest. This was why he was so wild. He was really alone with his terror.

At the end of my time with Emma, the year before I moved and closed my New Jersey practice, I worked very intensely with Benji and he changed and matured quite a bit. He was able to leave behind the constant flashback that had been his life. He grew and managed to have connection and co-operation with the others in the interests of bringing more stability to the whole system.

Unfortunately, months after we ended there was some regression. Ben did manage to stay out of flashback; he was no longer trapped in the days and nights of his horrifying memories. But neither Louie nor the others would listen to or accept Benji's memories. As a result, Benji began to make trouble for all of "system Emma." The cost to the system of not accepting Benji's memories was that he stayed very young and acted very rashly often putting Emma at risk. He gambled away large sums of money, for instance. I learned this many years after I moved and our work together had ended. That was when Emma emailed me and reluctantly asked for my help in finding another therapist. After many years of trying to suppress Benji and paying the price, Emma had resigned herself to going back into treatment. Hopefully the "greater Emma" would find a way to accommodate Benji and all of his memories.

chapter 11
listening is an act of love

"Listening is an act of love"
—David Isay, radio producer of StoryCorps,
NPR program and project

A year or two into Emma's treatment, my husband and I went on a bike tour of Provence.

The scenery was spectacular, the biking arduous. My back hurt, I didn't really like the people on the tour, there was too much food and wine. Nevertheless, it was a *terrific* vacation. Those endless Provençal hills, the intensely blue Van Gogh Sky, the Luberon Mountains, impressionistic scenery everywhere, the heavenly smell of rosemary and thyme hedges: they all served to drown out the noise of Emma constantly buzzing in my head. At that point she occupied the largest chunk of real estate in my mind. I needed some respite.

I don't think it was ever Emma's memories, recounted in vivid real time, i.e. flashbacks, that were so haunting and preoccupying. I think it was the privation of all the "children," the child parts within Emma, the constant pressure to find the right boundary to protect the treatment, to protect myself from burnout and what is variously called compassion fatigue, secondary traumatization, or vicarious traumatization.

How many out-of-session phone calls should I allow? Lengthy emails? Extended sessions? There were many "children" and most of them wanted my attention. Emma had been brutalized by people who knew no boundaries. Boundaries were important for her healing as well as for my own preservation.

Emma was actually more respectful of my need for limits and self-protection than were several other dissociative clients that I had over the years. She rarely pushed me beyond where I could go. She wasn't as entitled as some. But the work was depleting and exhausting nonetheless.

I relished the challenge of unpacking the complexity of Emma's system, the relationships within the system and their relationship to me. It was *totally* engaging. I loved that about the work. But engagement could become obsession if I didn't watch it. I needed space in my mind for things other than Emma and puzzling over the challenges that just kept coming and coming. How often should I see her? Was twice a week enough/too much? How could I best titrate memories that often came in a rush and threatened to overwhelm her? Should I support the marriage that provided her with some stability but was also quite problematic? Were her children safe from her more cruel and angry parts? It required a lot of mental and emotional energy to be Emma's therapist and I was often drained.

There were many, many crises and I would worry about Emma's well-being, her ability to keep herself safe. The responsibility weighed heavily on me. I was often trying to figure out what was going on behind the scenes, how to deal with difficult sub-personalities who challenged and undermined the treatment. Emma's many parts were often invested in maintaining their separate identities and they defended their turf to the detriment of the whole system. Joey resented how much time Louie took. Louie often muscled Joey off the stage and thus undermined the whole treatment. Often I doubted myself: did I have the competence to really help Emma? The treatment was so tumultuous, would she survive? Would I?

I have long been drawn to the story of Jacob wrestling with the Angel in Genesis. It is a story of transformation and of struggle. On the eve of a meeting with his long estranged brother, now enemy, Esau, Jacob dreams of a meeting with an Angel in which there is a wrestling match of sorts. The struggle ends in a tie; neither prevails. Jacob extracts a blessing from his adversary, who then renames him "Israel." Jacob is transformed by the struggle *and* he is physically wounded: "He injured the socket of Jacob's thigh, dislocating it as he wrestled with him."

Most biblical commentators, I am told, feel that this event fostered positive growth in Jacob. This is what I take from that story: struggle changes you. There is both a blessing and a lasting wound. I feel that way about Emma; working with her changed me for sure. I think there is more blessing than wound, but the wound is surely there. I probably still don't have enough distance to know exactly how the experience changed and/or wounded me. This book is my best effort at an honest assessment.

I did some research in the late '90s on trauma therapists. I interviewed eight experienced trauma therapists in depth, exploring their reactions to the work they did with patients. I was interested in learning if there were differences between experienced therapists who specialized in treating adult survivors of childhood abuse—particularly sexual abuse—who had had their own history of childhood abuse and those who stated that they had not. I was investigating the possibility of differences in the experience of vicarious traumatization in the two groups. These conditions refer to the negative effects on psychotherapists of doing long-term treatment with individuals with chilling tales to tell: tales of sadism and violence toward children.

I learned that the childhood history of my therapist-subjects was *not* an important variable, at least in my small study. There was evidence of negative effects on all the interviewees, but the picture that emerged was complex. Most of my interviewees felt that they had been changed by their work, but there were as many positive effects as negative. Many said they felt wiser, more mature and deeper, and they were grateful. They had had to dig something out of themselves to help their clients. They valued the mining of resources within and felt that it had made them more mature and wise human beings.

I, for one, learned more about darkness—about the psychopathic impulses of perpetrators—than I ever wished to know. But I also know that some people, like Emma, have steel in their bones and their souls, and can turn themselves inside out in order to live and grow. That is inspiring.

Whenever I walk through the Holocaust Museum here in DC, I find that I want to and sometimes do avert my gaze. A particular photograph is just too appalling to linger upon. I often avoid TV shows or movies where there will be violence, which is hard to do for there is so much of it. But when treating someone who has suffered so greatly, particularly as a child, you can't listen well to the patient and avoid the graphic details of violent abuse. A parent of youngish children myself at the time I worked with Emma, I wanted to avert my gaze from the images of her suffering, but I had to stay connected. One of my therapist interviewees described the conflict:

> I think there is just this physical reaction on my part, you know, I don't want to hear it. It feels very difficult to hear [of] a child being treated this way, so sadistically and so cruelly…it would set up my not asking enough questions about it probably, not wanting to hear it. I don't think I would actively stop somebody from talking about it but there's so much premeditation and evil in that and of course I know from studies that [this] heightens the effect of sexual abuse in terms of level of trauma. [She means that the intention of the perpetrator impacts the level of trauma.]

I was not so overwhelmed by Emma's testimony, though, for the most part. Its effect on me was more indirect. Emma's various identities, particularly in the early years, were very young children without parents. Their needs were enormous and legitimate given the deprivation they had experienced; however, they were often too much for a human therapist. I had to find the line, hold the line, set limits and boundaries to protect the treatment, to protect Emma and to protect myself. That was very difficult. I think I did less well with this than with shielding myself from absorbing the horror that was described. How does a therapist end a session on time when she has just witnessed a flashback, a re-enactment of a savage rape? How do you refuse calls on vacation when you know your client is in a suicidal crisis and no one around is really qualified to cover with this particular individual? Or was that just my grandiosity, thinking I was the only helper qualified?

Some of the therapists in my study reported being more cynical in their worldview as a result of the work they were doing with trauma patients. I think I was already pretty cynical. As a Jew who grew up in the 20th Century, I am quite aware of the atrocities that took place in Europe before I was born; they affected pretty much every Jew alive at that time. I never had trouble believing Emma's reports of sadism, brutality and ruthlessness.

I am accepting of the reality of darkness in the world, of evil, and also of resilience, our ability to survive and heal as Emma did. If her healing was not complete, neither was her shattering. She did put a lot of the pieces together and she has a life.

Some of the therapists I interviewed said they felt less safe in the world as a result of treating trauma patients. All expressed anger at the insensitivity to violence in our society and culture toward women and children, toward the vulnerable. One woman therapist said, "How do you live in a world where horrible things happen? How do you make peace with this? How do you forgive?"

I am not aware of an altered sense of safety for myself, but I was perhaps more aware, more protective and vigilant of my young daughters the more deeply I got into the work with severely traumatized patients. I could never take my children's safety for granted. I think they may have absorbed some of this but it tended to be expressed, in their teens, as a strong feminism. One daughter was a leading organizer of the "take-back-the-night" march at her college. My other daughter became a therapist and for a time worked with highly traumatized children.

Many of the subjects of my study mentioned how draining the work could be and how necessary it was for them to find ways to protect or renew themselves outside of their work with severely traumatized patients. Some therapists spoke of balancing their caseloads so that they weren't always working with trauma patients. Some spoke of putting more emphasis on rest, relaxation and recreation. I was aware myself of feeling depleted and outside of the trip to France, I did not win any awards for self-renewal. I *did* have regular individual and peer group supervision; I *did* do yoga and meditation regularly; and I had my own therapy. Nonetheless, I was in a solo practice in a home office much of this time, with no colleagues down the hall with whom to share experiences. Like so many others doing this difficult work, I told myself I was handling it fine. There were really no obvious signs within me of harmful effects, which is of course the problem: they are cumulative, implicit, insidious and below the level of consciousness. If I was drinking, I would have noticed that, but I wasn't. If I was not sleeping, I would have noticed that; disturbed sleep was not new to me. If I had bellyaches or headaches on work days, I would have noticed that too. None of this was happening. But I spent too much of *every* day puzzling over Emma and how best to treat her.

One interesting, perhaps important and definitely unexpected observation in my study was that several of my therapist subjects had physical ailments—like fibromyalgia—which today are understood to be associated with trauma and stress. Since the time I did this study (1998-9), many other studies have found a connection between stress and fibromyalgia as well as other poorly explained pain disorders. In the clinical journal *Psychotherapy and Psychosomatics*, B. Van Houdenhove noted, "Although the exact aetiology and pathogenesis of FM are still unknown, it has been suggested that stress may play a key role in the syndrome." (2004.) Other studies have linked fibromyalgia to adverse (read trauma) experiences in childhood. These ailments occurred in both the group describing themselves as abuse survivors and those who denied that specific history.

I myself have had and continue to have stress related difficulties such as back pain and a challenging digestive disorder, despite all my restorative efforts. It does seem that having spent decades bearing witness to extreme suffering day after day, year after year, not just with Emma, may have played some role in the genesis or exacerbation of those difficulties; but it's hard to know.

Despair is always lurking in this kind of treatment. It comes with the territory; the client has felt such despair in the original situation in childhood, trapped in a family that was either unwilling or unable to protect them from extreme harm. It is easily re-experienced in the treatment situation, both by patient and therapist. The therapist's job is to help the patient process and possibly repair horrible memories. But remembering feels like punishment sometimes and the therapist becomes the agent of that punishment: "You want me to remember? To tell you what happened? It is *awful* to remember! It is awful for me and it will be awful for you."

Sometimes it felt impossible to Emma and to me to find hope in the lean offerings of psychotherapy, which is at best an imperfect instrument for healing. I was keenly aware of that. And maybe, so was Emma.

My biggest problem—and this I shared with many of the subjects of my study—was the isolation I felt from colleagues and friends alike. Even colleagues didn't want to hear too much about what I was doing for a living. One member of my peer supervision group asked, "Could you be less detailed in your descriptions, please? It triggers me!" This meant I was holding these horrors all by myself. In retrospect, I probably shouldn't have been quite so accommodating. This *was* a supervision group and part of the implicit pact was to help each other shoulder the responsibilities of a caseload that at times could be crushing.

At the time I was treating Emma, particularly in the professional community where I treated Emma, there were not many therapists—or any—that worked with DID. Memories of abuse were under fire in the culture, in the media and even in the profession; all of which served to make me feel more alone professionally than I do today. Thirty years later and in the community in which I work now, DID is understood to be much more prevalent; there is more acceptance and training available. My peer supervision group and my supervisor got me through, but neither the group nor the supervisor had had direct experience or training in this work. I read all I could, I went to trainings and conferences, but it was lonely. It was as if Emma and I, and other DID patients that I worked with, existed in a bubble, a clandestine world only occasionally validated by the larger professional community.

In my study, it was surprising to me how frequently the therapist-subjects spoke of being enhanced rather than taxed by the work they were doing. This mirrored my own experience with Emma. These are some of the things they said:

"Working with survivors enhanced my self-esteem and is thereby emotionally satisfying."

"Empowering my survivor clients empowers me."

"It makes me feel hopeful to work with these clients."

"I feel creative in doing this work."

"It has increased my self-esteem as a professional."

"Working with survivors has helped in my own personal growth."

"I do better work with all of my patients."

I did feel that in working with dissociation, I had found my niche, something that I was really good at and could feel good about. I understood these clients and these processes. Figuring out what was often a thousand-piece puzzle was mostly a welcome challenge. The logic of dissociation seemed obvious to me: you are suffering and you find a way to not be there. The suffering is intense and prolonged and the "not being there" coalesces into an identity, or multiple identities. If the traumatizing events go on long enough all of this sticks and moves to automatic pilot.

It is not easy to gauge what changes were wrought by all my years with Emma. They were a large part of my "seasoning" as a psychotherapist. Maybe now I listen more acutely and stay more focused as a result of having to watch for switches in Emma's identities: "Who is here now?" Maybe I am more sensitive to the "parts" of my *non*-dissociative clients. I have found over the years that almost all my patients get it instantly when I speak of a child part of their self-organization, of a need for the adult part to help the child part.

I lead a weekly meditation group where I have been told there is a quality to my voice that helps people find the flow, the meditative state. I now wonder if I cultivated a vocal tone, "prosody" it's called, to soothe and comfort the most traumatized child parts of Emma.

There were many heart-warming moments, whole phases of work with Emma that were nourishing. Louie, at age 10, brought me things he made for me in a crafts class that he took: a hanger for my keys still nailed up in my closet now, a froggie clipboard that still organizes the papers on my desk. Nan, the artistic twin, drew a picture of Louie and me fishing together, a pencil sketch of a wish he had always had, that we would go fishing together. Through the drawing he got some measure of the gratification that his therapist could not fully provide. It was very sweet and I still have it hanging in my office. These items made the move with me with me from NJ to DC. They are part of the "permanent collection."

Louie had often fancied himself as the son I never had. This was nice for me too. He was at once exasperating and endearing, frustrating and fun. In later years, when Louie grew into more of the CEO of "system Emma" and became more rigid, argumentative and controlling, there were other boys containing other aspects of Emma's memory system: the creative, joyous energy that survived the private Holocaust of Emma's childhood. They loved the out-of-doors, animals, fishing, boating, exploring the natural world. In the garden, in the woods, on the lake, with the dogs they felt safe. The girls were softer, more cerebral: thinkers, readers, nurturers. I could depend on the girls to take care of the younger child parts.

Having known Emma, I am more aware of how enhanced we all are if we have access to many parts of ourselves: the boy parts, the girl parts, the joyous and the reflective. Access and integration both lead to a greater wisdom and a greater flexibility, an enriched humanity.

What I learned from Emma and gained as a person as well as a therapist far outweighs the costs, the wounds that I suffered.

Even as I struggled biking up those hills in France, I would sometimes be filled with joy. I remember saying to nobody in particular, "I could die among the sea of sunflowers growing here and I would be happy: a dream fulfilled." This trip was something I had always wanted to do, ever since I was a teenager, and now I was finally doing it! Alas, I was no longer a teenager; the hills got increasingly more challenging for me as the trip progressed and fatigue set in. At least once I cried from the effort of it and the feeling I was no match for the steep terrain. But as I wrote in my journal: "It has been a great experience, physically exhausting but mentally restful." I was truly on vacation.

chapter 12
sydney and emma

The day I read my first draft of this chapter to my writing group, I sobbed. It had been at least six years since Sydney died. I had written and rewritten the draft, sitting at my computer dry-eyed. But when I read it aloud I could not finish. My heart was still broken and I did not know it. This too is dissociation.

Today I am trying to decide what to do about telling Emma that Sydney is dying. Sydney, my dear friend, for several years, my co-therapist in a women's therapy group in which Emma and all of her part-selves were participants, has been dying for some time, but now we know it's near the end.

My friend Dean, also a therapist, has just asked me if/when I am going to tell Emma; for she is sure to find out soon. I had not planned on complicating our work by sharing this difficult information. The group in which the two of them, Sydney and Emma, were deeply engaged ended many years ago. Although our social circles do not intersect, at least as far as I know, Dean points out that Emma knows people who would soon know.

As it turned out, this was Sydney's very final day.

Many years before, I had convinced Emma to join a therapy group for women who had childhood histories of sexual abuse. I did not yet

105

know that Emma had many part-selves, that she was DID. Had I known, I would not have taken the risk of introducing that kind of chaos into the group. But I did and chaos happened. As soon as Emma "outed" herself in the group, we suddenly had several highly dissociated women who also had successfully hidden their diagnoses from their respective therapists, notably me. In retrospect, it is not surprising that a group of women who had experienced betrayal and abuse—some of them repeatedly, violently, sadistically at the hands of family members and clergy as very young children—would be dealing with some degree of dissociation. I was not seasoned enough to know that. Emma had not yet fully educated me.

When Emma was ready to talk to the group at large about her parts, at least two other women outed themselves as well. Sydney and I were stunned; and our work became more difficult. Knowing there were other "children" in the group empowered a few other "children" in the group to appear and act out. Adolescent part-selves came to group high on marijuana. Sometimes they held meetings at the local coffee shop to ridicule and trash the two therapists.

Sydney and I co-led the group for five years. Emma knew Sydney well. Rebellious, soon-to-be- adolescent Louie and Sydney had often clashed in the group. Early on, when I had taken a week's vacation and Sydney handled the group alone, Louie and Sydney had a loud confrontation, with Louie calling Sydney "stupid and fake." Sydney was more straight-laced than I and Louie just loved to goad her. Sydney actually threw something at him once. He deserved it.

Sydney and I had been very involved in each other's personal lives as well. When we all met at a wedding, close to the end of her life, Syd moved close to my youngest daughter, tears in her eyes, and told her, "I knew you before you were born." And she had, having directed me to the doctor who successfully delivered her.

Tiny, slim, striking, elegant, always stylish, Sydney's clothes were classy and beautiful. As the rest of us sagged into our middle age and beyond, Sydney grew more striking: blond became silver, pretty became beautiful. The scarf, the necklace, the expensive but never flashy jewelry;

the house and yard of which she was so proud, impeccably and tastefully decorated and cultivated.

She had an artist's aesthetic; both her house and her outward appearance were her canvas. She judged others according to her high standards; even her case presentations inevitably began with a vivid, detailed depiction of her patient's exterior presentation, clothes, hair, age, demeanor. I was keenly aware of Sydney's judgment of *my* appearance and *my* house as well. Once, as we entered a party room together, Sydney physically recoiled at the garish colors and rather tasteless "theme" of the affair: "Oh, no!" She later recanted, realizing her reaction was rather harsh, but it was a reflex, not calculated.

Many people found Syd cold and not a few asked me how I could be so close to someone so distant. I thought I could get underneath that chill often enough to make the friendship viable. Sometimes I could, sometimes I couldn't.

Sydney was very smart and very committed to her work. She would not give in to discomfort and showed up for her patients throughout her chemotherapy and radiation treatments, rarely taking a day off. She only retired when it became impossible to function well and be fully present for her patients.

Sydney was proud. She held herself rather stiffly but always with dignity. I believe it was a profound humiliation for her to have had a cancer that was eating her up, altering her appearance and even her voice, her perfect presentation to the world.

Sydney, like all of us, had many parts. Some of her parts were wise, funny, honest and warm. Some were rigid, chilly, insecure and even rejecting. I was drawn to the former, often tormented by the latter.

When she died, I had known Sydney for at least 30 years. We had been co-therapists in two groups, a support group for mothers of newborns, and the therapy group in which Emma was a key player. We had also been together for decades in a peer supervision group. For better or for worse, our lives were braided together for the biggest chunk of our respective adulthoods.

*Today's session begins with the adult Emma in the room. We
are chatting about current events, i.e. hers, when Emma
starts: "I hear a loud bang inside," and there is a sudden
switch, an unusual occurrence in our work together. She
slowly sinks to the floor, a clear signal that the smaller,
younger child parts will come forward with their memories.
I almost see what is happening within her. She is writhing
on my rug. A parade, a chaotic procession of small children
are here, stunned, frightened, bewildered and then grief
stricken. I am witnessing a reliving, a re-enactment of
Joey's death, a tragic piece of Emma's earlier history…a
history I have long known about, and recounted earlier.
Now I am an eyewitness.*

It only took a few minutes, this re-enactment, and I understood.
Each one of Emma's child parts had a characteristic posture, facial
expression, evoked a signature bodily sensation within me and after so
many years of working with Emma, I didn't need words of introduction to recognize the swift changes within her, from fear to shock to
devastation, each emotion embodied differently and spilling onto my
rug. It was a little like watching a silent movie, without the subtitles; it
was clear what is going on, although there was no spoken narrative. I
knew enough of the plot to guess what was occurring.

When we are undergoing a rush of powerful emotions, we uncon-
sciously signal this to others with subtle and not so subtle facial and
postural changes. We communicate with each other with these visual
cues as well as with changes in voice quality and tone. This is what was
happening in my office with Emma and all her splintered, shattered
child parts who had witnessed the horror of the sudden death of *her* best
friend. All the self-splinters that resulted from that witnessing, from that
terrible loss, presented themselves virtually at my feet: a vivid, visceral,
re-experiencing of the sudden death of Emma's six-year old chum Joey
as he was hit by a car, less than a mile from where we now sat, while
the two children played together. The loud bang that Emma heard at

the beginning of the dramatic re-enactment was the collision of the car and the body of her little friend.

It may be that this one re-enactment in my office and our shared shock and grief helped Emma to consolidate some of the splintering she experienced at the time of Joey's sudden death, for I never saw nor heard from these fragmentary ego states again. In any case, I was stunned by the drama of what had just occurred in the session. In her own way, Emma intuited what is happening to me regarding Sydney, maybe understanding it more fully that I did.

The system, "greater Emma," had somehow sensed my sadness, my grief, through the medium of dissociated memory. Emma knew that Sydney and I were close and that losing her would be to lose one of my dearest friends. While the adult Emma (and Louie) did not have the information about Sydney's impending death, the kaleidoscope of shattered child part-selves within Emma already knew the emotional truth, on their deeper, dissociated level, in a way that was cataclysmic to them. To not confirm their reality would have been to repeat the abuse, to deny truth and their experience. Denial of the truth is one of the reasons Emma was in so many pieces. Multiplicity is sometimes the only way to both hold on to knowledge and to keep the secret. "System Emma" had decided for me; I had to tell her.

No more dithering. "Emma," I said, "Please come forward. I need to talk to you. Sydney is in the hospital, she is dying. You have just shown me," I explained, "that you know and also what this was like for you, that it was shattering. You are trying to understand some of what I feel."

The adult Emma, and now adult Louie (at this point in the treatment he had caught up in age with Emma) were stunned. Interestingly, Louie, who fought with Sydney all those years ago, was the most distraught. He claimed, "I always liked her, liked her spirit."

Many months after Sydney's death, one of Emma's clairvoyant parts told me that she had dreamed of Sydney walking along with her "red dog" and that Sydney was happy. Emma claimed never to have seen Sydney with her real "red dog," a golden retriever that had long since left this earth. Emma understood this dream to be a message from "the other side." She may have seen Sydney walking Jack in healthier times and "forgotten" or dissociated the memory, but I must say I am comforted by the idea that Jack is on the other side to greet and love Sydney. Emma gave me a gift.

After the immediate shock passed, Emma, the adult, a health care professional who knew about death and dying, urged me to go and say goodbye. "She is in a coma, near death" I said, "and I have not been invited by the family. It feels intrusive." That my friend and I had a complicated relationship, I did not share.

Emma now counseled me, our roles changed in the midst of this crisis. She had cared for many patients at the end of their lives. "Even in a coma she will hear you, hearing is the last thing to go. It's really important to her that you go!" She was insistent.

It took awhile but eventually I was persuaded. I cancelled the rest of my day and I went.

Sydney, no longer Sydney—petite, bloated, diminished, distorted in the process of dying, no longer the lovely, proud, in-control Sydney—was lying in bed, barely covered by a hospital gown, softly groaning. Was this the death rattle? I was overwhelmed to see and hear this beautiful woman to whom I had been attached over so much of my adult life, transfigured, transformed in the agony of dying. The room was actually crowded with friends and family that *had* been invited to say goodbye and I found there was no place to hide my sobs. Sydney's husband moved some visitors aside so that we, a few friends from the peer supervision group, could sit close to her for a few minutes. Her left hand twitched; I grabbed it as if summoned. I held her hand: "We love you, I love you." To this day, I fervently hope that she heard.

That night she passed away.

In my album of remembered images of our long friendship, I can still see our peer supervision group at Sydney's dining room table on Friday mornings, amidst coffee and bagels, always a generous breakfast at Sydney's house. We met as a group for more than 20 years. It was in that group that we sorted out together how to treat Emma, how to manage the child version of Louie and his shenanigans, how to understand the twists and turns and turbulence of Emma's system struggling to give up her horrendous secrets. On many occasions, the cast of characters that comprised the "greater Emma" was as vivid to my group as it was to me. I don't think I could have managed without this group. They didn't question the veracity of her reportage; they didn't challenge me for believing the grisly, brutal reports of pitiless abuse that I was hearing. They were right there with me.

It was so painful to see and hear Sydney in her final hours. It took many years before I was glad that I went to the hospital that day. But I am glad now.

This is but one instance in which it is clear that the guidance, the counsel and the comfort that one has with certain patients goes in both directions. In the best of psychotherapy treatments, healing is bi-directional.

> *The day of the funeral I sat dry-eyed throughout the service, aware of the people around me, friends, former friends, colleagues, Sydney's family. I listened to the eulogies. Dry-eyed. As we filed out, I heard a baby cry, probably held by a parent at the back of the chapel. Only then did tears begin to flow. This too is dissociation.*

chapter 13
here comes goodbye

Here comes goodbye, here comes the last time
Here comes the start of every sleepless night
The first of every tear I'm gonna cry
Here comes the pain, here comes me wishing things had never changed
And she was right here in my arms tonight, but here comes goodbye
—Rascal Flatts. This was one of Louie's songs
from the CD compilation that Emma
and her parts gave me when we ended.

It started to rain heavily, torrentially, soon after we left Wesleyan. We could hardly see a few yards ahead. There was a bike rack atop our car since we had dropped her bike off along with many of her worldly goods. The seal where the bike rack was affixed to the car roof was not tight; water dripped relentlessly into the car.

My firstborn was off to college and freshman orientation had begun; also my mourning. Actually, I had begun mourning at least a year before, anticipating the revolutionary changes to come, the change in the daily-ness of our family life. No meals together, no goodnight hugs at bedtime, no sharing of family and friend gossip, no hectoring about homework. Such an unnatural occurrence, shipping our young people off to college at various distances. Not every affluent western country does this. I understand they don't do this in Canada. Was it too late to move?

As is her wont, my sturdy, adventurous first born sailed happily into her new life with nary a glance backward. We had just re-enacted her first day of kindergarten.

Our family had moved to a neighboring town so that Sarah could go to a better kindergarten back in 1980. She would attend public school finally, traveling on the classic big yellow bus. The mothers and a few fathers were gathered at the bus stop, just across the street from our house, with cameras and Kleenex boxes and younger toddlers in tow. I scoffed inwardly.

My daughter had gone to nursery school very happily at two and a half, and had banged on the screen door to go out and play with the big kids from the time she could stand upright. Mother and child were both old hands at this. I felt superior. No biggie. No camera, no Kleenex. I was new in the neighborhood but recognized a few people who were also launching their firstborns. But they felt the drama much more than I. I knew how to do this, confident that this was just another necessary step in my daughter's development and my increased freedom.

The bus came and very quickly scooped up our children. Sarah hopped on with ease, marched quickly toward the back of the bus, not a backward glance or a wave. It all happened in an instant and she was off. Gone. I looked around quickly; who had kicked me in the stomach? Oh, God. No tears, just the ground giving way, and this pain in my stomach. The body knows, even as the mind dissembles. This was not nursery school. This was the big time. There was a bus involved.

But 12 years later, dropping Sarah off at college, body and mind were one, right along with the weather. It was pouring rain and I *was* crying. This seemed like the ultimate launching. It seems clearer to me now that the pain with which I approached and experienced this event was strongly influenced by my own launching 30 years earlier, when *I* started college.

I alone among my friends from high school chose to go to a college many miles from home. With so many good New England schools to choose from, much closer to home and family, I chose Antioch in the southwest corner of Ohio. Nine hundred miles was a lot further away than it is now; we drove or we took a bus, very little airplane travel was involved. I was attracted to Antioch for a number of reasons, but its distance from home and family might have been the most compelling one. A good friend from high school with whom I reconnected and compared notes 50 years after our graduation remembers that I told her I *wanted* to go far away.

But as my family drove away, the full enormity of my choice settled in. I remember vividly how hollowed out and scared I was. I looked around at the featureless Midwestern landscape: no briny smell on the wind, no access to Maine lobster, the beach and my beloved New England rocky coast. I never stopped missing that place. Even now, 50 years later, I will turn a corner, not really present to the moment, and for a fraction of a second think I am turning onto Pilgrim Road, just around the corner from the house in which I grew up. Somewhere inside me I am still walking to Eaton's drugstore, which no longer exists, and enjoying the smells of corned beef and pickled tongue at Beach Bluff Deli, which also no longer exists.

My closest friends were very far away and the foreignness of the bohemian student body—dirty feet in scuffed sandals, boys with long oily hair and beards—scared me. I wondered if I would ever fit in. This scruffy bunch represented a culture that was alien to me, an early 1960s teenager. Flower children, unfettered sexuality, drugs, radical politics: they all came early to Antioch and I was not so ready for them. I was looking not for the Haight-Ashbury ethos, but for distance and a chance to grow into myself far from the overbearing, oppressive, controlling, soul-crushing atmosphere of home. I would miss my siblings and long for my mother, but I desperately needed to *breathe* away from my father. It was all a muddle at the time, but I knew that I would not have much of a self if I didn't leave. And leave I did, not really ever to return.

The car trip out to Ohio was long and tense. My father was always wound extra tight on car trips. Although my mother was quite capable of driving and drove at home all the time, she didn't drive on the highway, at least on long trips. My father was always the pilot, she the navigator.

One scene jumps out at me most forcefully from that trip; it served to underscore how vital it was to me to get away, far away: we were in Ohio, still a few hours away from arriving at my college. Cornfield after cornfield provided the only scenic distraction. I was sitting in the backseat with my siblings, who were also tense and definitely bored. My father asked what language classes I planned on taking in the coming year or two. As is probably the case with most not-quite-freshman in college, I had given virtually *no* thought to this or any other academic choices that would face me soon. With a mental shrug, I answered, "German," only because it was the language choice that had the most cachet in my high school. The smartest kids took German; it was thought to be harder to learn than the Romance languages. I had taken lots of Latin and French in high school, but wasn't looking to continue either one. My father exploded, "You idiot!" cursing me, furious that I would aspire to learn the language of the people who had murdered millions of Jews. It was my father's tone more than the words that had always scared me. When he got angry there was no modulation, no self-restraint. He was screaming at me. He reacted as if this was a personal and enraging rejection of him. I still quake a little at the memory.

At that time I had no idea that the Nazis had murdered his mother and sister. Maybe I would have been more careful had I known this, but probably not. I don't think we ever discussed the Holocaust and its impact on him, on our family history. I had no context for this rage at the German language. It was just a language that you took when you had to take language course.

The words and the issue were new but the melody was oh so familiar: an explosion that was triggered by my choices, my opinions. In this case it was completely unexpected. So close to the end of our car journey, so close to the final separation, this incident was tailor made to seal the deal: I had to get away.

Was I thinking about my getaway, my journey away from my family, as we rolled away from Sarah, a teenager not anything like me at that age? No, not really. She was not particularly scared. She was ready and she was very excited, charging forward with boundless, heedless eagerness. College was freedom from oversight, a chance to try her wings, but it was not a loss of connection. She did not need to go so very far away to grow into herself. The world felt safe to her, or at least safe enough. She would wrestle with issues of autonomy and connection as much as any child of her age would, but it was not a Hobson's choice for her, family/home vs. self, as it had been for me.

No, I was not *consciously* thinking of my own wobbly launch. There was just a weirdly overwhelming grief. Sarah's experience was not really parallel to mine. But some younger, still bereft, teenage part of me lurking silently within was still grieving my own losses as I went off to college, never to return in any meaningful way to my family, to my hometown, or even my high school friends. In retrospect, I think that teenager part *was* quaking with fear that history would repeat itself and my daughter would have to leave me too…and that would be a loss I could not bear.

Sarah's separations—kindergarten and college—and mine seem like reasonable examples of two distinctly different solutions to the challenging task of coming into one's own, becoming a young adult. Perhaps I flatter myself as a parent, but Sarah's very joyous entry to kindergarten and college point to a securely attached child launching from a secure base. She knew we would be there to hug her upon her return. My own separations were more problematic. I needed to get away in order to be myself. My solution was to get far away, move away and become as independent as I could manage at a very young age.

And then there is Emma. Clearly her history of attachments and separations were so much more problematic than mine. It is possible that very early on, Emma's mother tried to watch out for her. But trauma so often—maybe always—occurs in a field of neglect, physical and/or emotional absence. "The worst things happened when mother would leave us," wrote Emma shortly after I announced I would be closing my practice in NJ. "Your leaving will help us remember more of that. And that is an opportunity.

At first, Emma *definitely* did not see this as an opportunity. At the beginning of October 2009, I told Emma and others that I would be closing my practice in New Jersey in nine months. I would be moving to the DC area to be closer to children and grandchildren. Emma was understandably shaken and angry. She wrote the next day:

> *I understand and accept the changes in your life and I am sorry for my anger yesterday, but I never saw this coming so I was hurt…. You taught me how to trust myself so I will do my best to work with the fallout. I can't see you for the next 10 months knowing that we have to race to get better because this is the end for all of us. We are all grateful for you 20 plus years that you have given 110%….* **I am not coming back because it hurts way too much. This is the pain I was scared of if I had a mother she will leave.** *[Emphasis is mine. Louie, who wrote the email, believed that Emma's biological parents were not his parents]. You are not my mother and we will part ways and maybe we will be friends in heaven someday? I can't get better in 10 months it's too hard…. I can't let you help me because the pain of losing you is too hard (unbearable.)*

As the reader has learned in the previous pages, Emma's trauma—physical, sexual, emotional—started at an early age, continued until she was about 15, and was both repetitive and severe. In guiding Emma back to treatment now. Angel noted: "You will remember the worst of the worst because May is leaving now." Angel, the wisest part of Emma, did see my goodbye as an opportunity. But many other parts shrank away and were terribly frightened and hurt.

Despite Emma's disastrous history, she had been able to attach and work with me over a very long period of time. She had left an abusive marriage and had settled down with a woman who was kind and forgiving; she has maintained that relationship for decades despite many challenges. The history of one's primary and early connections frames the rest of life. This is pretty much a settled fact in child development theory. A secure base allows for a steady, happy launch. A wobbly base might haunt one forever in the absence of corrective experiences later in life. Psychotherapy is one of those potentially remedial experiences. A good marriage/partnership is another. When early experiences fail to protect the young child from cruelty, pain and fear, and when there is no basic safety in the early years, we expect to see fearfulness and often an inability to attach. Emma's inner selves provided attachment opportunities. They were her adaptation to all the lacunae in her life. Angel was her abiding friend. Emmie and Joey always had each other. The twins were…twins.

Emma convinced herself that she had had irreparable harm to her attachment equipment. "I don't attach," she said. "Out of sight out of mind." She tended to keep to herself and not make many friends. However, when her beloved dog died recently, she grieved deeply and painfully, and for many, many months she had great difficulty re-attaching to the new puppies. In this she saw her scarred capacity to love. She loved the deceased dog passionately though, and perhaps rolled into that love and grief were other lost loves, perhaps even the loss of her own childhood. She hurt so deeply because she *was* intensely attached, both to the dog and to me. She was scared to risk her heart again. But I believe she will.

I knew that Emma needed more time and that she would reject the idea of working with someone else, but it was the right time to move for me personally and for my family. My husband had the opportunity to retire in a good circumstance and it felt like a chapter was closing in our lives in our community. Only now do I notice that it was about a year after Sydney's death that our plans began to gel and the decision to leave moved forward. Perhaps that event had hastened our departure. I had previously thought I could never move from my lovely Victorian home, leave my *finally* mature and luxuriant garden; then almost overnight I wanted to move out of my house and was even ready to leave my garden, reluctant but ready. I thought I could never close my practice and say goodbye to all the clients that I was so attached to; suddenly it became possible to think about closing my practice. I thought I couldn't leave the support and nourishment of my community and friends and then, with regret but determination, we decided to leave the community and try to maintain friendships at a distance.

There would be many losses for my husband and me, but we knew we needed to turn the page. And we did.

The reality that I was "only a therapist," not a life companion, hit Emma hard. I once said to another client who was demanding more than I could give "I am what I am, only a therapist." She wryly deemed it the "Popeye defense." And so it was. "I yam what I yam and dat's all dat I yam," sayeth Popeye. My ties to Emma were and still are deep and strong. This project is testimony to that fact. But her ties to me were of a different nature, and it shook her hard when she realized I would go.

I replied to her email:

> *All of your goodbyes to people you really loved and depended on were traumatic, starting with the sudden violent death of (Joey).... And then his family left abruptly and without a goodbye. Additionally I think you were told not to talk about or even think about him. Then there was Mom—one time she did walk out for several days and leave you with Daddy who you feared might well kill you in her absence. [Other times] she left for long horrible periods as well, leaving you in the hands of tormenters and abusers.*
>
> *I fear that if you leave suddenly like this, without any talking, processing, reminiscing, explaining, hugging, whatever we need to do, we will have a repeat performance and another trauma.... While I well understand the need to take control over something that you feel is out of your control and try to cauterize the pain by doing so, I think it will not be good for*

you. It will not be a therapeutic farewell but a rather traumatic one (believe it or not there are therapeutic farewells!). This is my understanding of why people need to take time to grieve their losses. The mind and body need time to catch up to the shock of a loss.

One month later, Emma did return and we worked fairly fruitfully for the nine months remaining. What is so special about Emma and others like her is that remnant of resilience; a determination to do and be better always won out. It was always a struggle but there it was.

At first Emma would not tell me what prompted her return, but eventually:

Angel told me that the hardest work was ahead and that we wouldn't do the hardest work until we were leaving. The worst things happened when mother would leave us. Your leaving will help us remember more of that. And that is an opportunity.

In the dream Angel showed me what would happen if we missed this opportunity to do our work. It was a room of 'missed opportunities.' The feeling there in the room was of deep despair. They were all studying up on their missed opportunities.

The image of a room of "missed opportunities" is so very compelling. It was to Emma and it still is to me.

So little of that last year of work remains in my memory. The early years are crisp and clear for me, but that last year, not so much. In my personal life I was distracted by the challenge of selling our house in a deteriorating housing market. The economics of our move would be more challenging because of the very soft market. There was much to be done to prepare for the sale. And on Emma's side, she was distracted, consumed with the diagnosis of her partner with an aggressive form of cancer and later, with the harsh treatments and side effects.

Benji did most of the work in the last months, taking me to the site of Emma's most devastating memories in which she witnessed a child's kidnapping and murder. This was hard on everyone as the memories leaked into the whole system, a prelude to more integration, an integration that they really weren't ready for. Ultimately the work had to be left unfinished.

Joey fought hard to find a way to continue the treatment long distance, via the internet, Skype or FaceTime. I did not think that was doable. I didn't really know where my husband and I would land, or even if I would start a practice, have an office, have a license to practice. And Emma's needs could not be easily met over the internet. I did leave the door open for occasional emails, but after I left that was evidently vetoed by the system. It was years before I heard from Emma again and that was a request to help her find another therapist.

This is what I wrote after reading her emails

Feb. 16, 2016

As I type away, struggling to bring Emma to the page, working on my opus, the real Emma appears in my inbox: 'I've found you!' she writes, as if this has been a difficult process. Maybe the difficulty was within her, for my website is pretty straightforward, I am eminently Google-able and my email address never changed. After nearly six years of self-imposed silence (I always made it clear I would be fine with hearing from her via email occasionally), Emma has reached out. She signs the email from the four most adult ego states.

It is both shocking and a bit exciting to hear from her. My respiration quickens and my heart pounds. I am so surprised and I have to admit a bit delighted. Emma is so in my head and now she is here in my inbox. There is a bit of a disconnect: she does not sound in the email exactly as she does in the pages of my memoir. To some extent I have idealized her.

She has had a difficult few years, she writes; she has been pretty ill (physically) and had a horrendous, almost fatal response to medications. The illness is part of the legacy of her abuse. She sends a picture of a much transformed woman, 30 lbs. heavier, seemingly many years older. She is surprised that I am 70; I am surprised that she is 52.

Emma contacted me looking for a therapist. This is great news! She resisted all attempts to connect her with another therapist before I left. Swearing there would never be anyone as wonderful as I etc., etc.

I am amazed at how rapidly I am drawn in—my assignment is merely to help her find her a therapist within a reasonable distance from her home in New Jersey. But I have to beat down every impulse to make 'interventions.' She speaks about how dispirited she is by her remaining symptoms, how troubled by Ben (aka Benji now a little older I gather), ghastly memories and I feel a little disheartened. I am tempted to make an email interpretation (like, 'you know you can't be at peace until you make peace with Ben'). She assures me that the parts are pretty co-operative with each other; everyone but Ben, who of course is raising holy hell. This is the cost, and it's a heavy one, of casting off a part of oneself.

I am amazed at how instantly reactive I am, wanting to rush in and fix—putting too much time into finding her someone, getting discouraged myself too quickly. What if I can't find her a good therapist? How guilty, all over again I am that I left her before she was truly and fully finished.

The good news, and it is fantastic news, really is that she wants to find a new therapist.

She talks about coming to DC to see me, but dissuades herself in the next sentence, she knows this is not really an option.

In the end, after five days, a therapist that she knows from couples work that she did with her partner finds her someone, someone she feels she can trust.

I fear she will pull out of the process, sabotage, or give up prematurely. I hope she won't. But I have a weird feeling about the whole thing: I am no longer irreplaceable...she has replaced me. Deflation. She actually says, 'Thank you, thank you,' but it really sounds like 'goodbye.'

I have the impression from the email exchange in 2016 that there are only five ego states left—four adults and Benji, who lives in exile from the greater Emma as his memories are unable to be borne by the rest. I don't really know how many there were to begin with; it was always a shifting number, but at least three times the number that Emma counts now. The number of ego states a patient has is equal to the challenges of dealing with horrendous, overwhelming memory. Fewer ego states indicate fewer challenges, more stability.

Benji's memories were the last pieces that Emma needed to address and this was why she asked for help in finding a therapist. It was also clear from the email exchange that my leaving had repercussions that I dread lingering upon. I also mentioned in the email exchange that I was in the process of trying to write a book about some of our experiences together.

Emmie, who is now the same age as Emma, writes:

> *[Louie] has really shut the world out since we ended therapy i think [reading the book] it might be comforting? [Louie] has changed how he feels about [Benji] and is very protective now of him. He is not the old [Louie] that you remember. He really keeps us away from much of the outside world. I don't mind that so much. [Joey] is a bit more outgoing. I guess that we have done the best we can with the cards we were dealt?*
>
> *We hit the big 50! except for Benji. Louie doesn't fish anymore and we are all struggling to connect with the 2 new puppies we now have. I guess the grief over losing Harvey [their beloved dog] has rocked our world in a way that is very foreign to us all? I honestly have never experienced Louie so grief stricken, It's kinda scary? God he loved that dog like no other, and losing him was more awful than we expected. Louie always said without Harvey there is NO air! Boy was he right about that. I am so happy you have 5 grandchildren! We have none. I wish you and your family all the best. Louie won't be mad about the book, he just doesn't want to feel hurt anymore. Losing you was something*

that he held his feelings inside about. His way is not my way. I do talk about it a lot with R. [her partner] and she has been a great comfort. We will be ok and please do what you feel is best with regards to the book.

So they are much more integrated than in days of yore, but there is still depression, some withdrawal from the world, and memories that cannot be assimilated.

There is a special intimacy between therapist and patient/client, particularly when the work is as intense and of long duration as it was with Emma. It was hard for me to leave her and move on to where my life's journey was taking me. It was and is still hard not to feel somehow accountable for her continuing difficulties. I can only hope that she will find the right fit with a therapist in the future and take the next steps. I hope Angel will remind them all of the "room of missed opportunities."

chapter 14

"disappeared david"— how I became a trauma therapist, part 2

I was helping my mother clean closets. The closets in my parent's bedroom had built in cabinets, way, way up high for storage. For some reason there was a box on the bed from that high up place. I was looking through and I found bundled up letters addressed to my father from someone I had never heard of. There was something strange about them and the tone was intimate, but I didn't recognize the sender. Maybe I noted an honorific but didn't recognize what it was. I asked my mother who this was, this stranger who seemed to have an important if undefined relationship with my father. Her answer was deeply unsatisfying and familiar: "I'll tell you when you're older." I was probably eight or nine at the time. "Older" came nine or 10 years later and was pretty much an accident.

On the way west to my first year of college in Ohio, we stopped in Chicago to visit cousins, never before mentioned to me or my siblings, never mentioned or seen afterwards. To this day I'm not sure how we are related to each other. Sitting around a large table with these newly discovered cousins, our very warm, genial cousin-host asked my father if he ever heard from his brother David. Who? What? There was another

sibling in the U.S., someone I had never heard of? It never occurred
to our cousin that my father's children would not know about David.

There were eight children in my father's family. I had assumed all
but one, my Auntie Mary, had perished back in Russia.

That box on the bed briefly (literally) out of the closet held letters
from David. As we sat at the table, the story, or some version of the
story, emerged. My father had an older brother who had come to the
U.S. long before he did, renounced his religion, his Jewish origins, and
became a Protestant minister. Something that I didn't understand was
said about his falling in with "that (Christian) crowd at the YMCA,"
maybe in Chicago, and about his ditching responsibilities to his family,
which somehow explained—or didn't explain—"disappeared David."
The story was muddled at the time and is still somewhat muddled in
my mind. He changed his last name, no longer the same as ours, and
I was never able to learn much more about him. My lack of curiosity
about all of this puzzles me deeply. I never followed up on this accidental
disclosure. I regret this profoundly.

It was never hard for me to grasp the idea of sequestered part-selves,
the legacy of trauma. I had almost instinctively understood what was
going on with patients who employed a high degree of dissociation to
make their way in the world. They too put things in a box, hid them
deep in a dark closet way up high, out of sight and out of mind. What
they put in their boxes, though, were parts of themselves: selves that held
stories of horrendous childhood trauma. And, unlike my father, they did
not have access to this long-term storage without intensive treatment.

The story of "disappeared David" popped up in my memory
recently as I listened to the elegant memoir of a colleague who spent
years piecing together the biography of her mother, a resistance fighter
in the Polish underground during the Second World War. I hadn't
thought about the incident in Chicago and the lost uncle in decades.
The re-emergence of this David- memory sent me back to a rough
memoir that my father had written in 1987; he was around 80 years
old. Maybe there was more about David in there.

Sadly, although there were indeed some early memories of David, the story of his conversion and separation from the family was missing. What I did encounter were fragmentary tales of the horrendous trauma that my father had experienced as a child. He recounts repeated dislocations within Russia, the country of his birth, the early death of an older brother and his revered father from typhoid. The years of the Russian revolution are filled with extreme violence, starvation, and barely acknowledged fear. Neither I nor my siblings had ever heard reference to incidents like the ones below.

> One couple with their young daughter, probably 10 or 12 years old, were dragged out of their apartment building into the street and shot right there. Blood was oozing out from their bodies. The young girl was left alive. For a moment she looked calm and still, almost frozen in place. Then she fell to the ground on the top of their bodies with an almost inhuman shriek.... The girl went berserk. She tore off her clothes and ran. Where to? I left the window, which was my observation point, and related the incident to the rest of the family. My mother yelled at me. I was told to stay away from the window or I would get killed. End of that incident. The next morning I forgot all about it (!). [Emphasis mine.]

There are more disturbing, and partially dissociated events that my father witnessed and he notes that he had "forgotten" about them until writing this history. How eerie to realize that my own father had perfected the art of dissociation: sequestering, "forgetting" the horrendous events he had witnessed. From his memoir:

> One night there was a knock at the door. Two uniformed red guards arrested our boarder. We never saw him again. No one ever claimed his belongings. One more bloodied occurrence. Whatever I related now is the way I saw it with the eyes of a young boy, who by now is immune to the most horrible sights. A similar hardened immunity was the armor that probably helped some of the Jews in the concentration camps to survive where mass executions were part of a horrible daily routine.

* * *

It was on one of the rare occasions when I was allowed to play in the street that a caravan of military trucks were rolling by. Soldiers in the leading truck were shooting in the air, aim[ing] to disperse the crowd. People ran to hide in doorways, patios, away from the shooting. But a stupid kid, like me stood there curiously trying to see what this was all about. Yes, I did see. I saw dead bodies piled up in [the] open truck, maybe 20 or 30 with heads and limbs swinging from the motion of the truck.

Looking through the window of time and observing the young boy watching the caravan of death roll by, detached, satisfying his curiosity of the event, void of other emotions. Probably a little scared.

After my paternal grandfather's untimely death, the family moved back to the city of my father's birth, Pinsk, which had become part of Poland. A cool, unaccommodating reception by his maternal grandparents and extended family eventually led to another emigration, to Cuba. This time he went alone. He was 15 ½ years old.

Disappeared David was but the tip of an iceberg concealing significant early trauma. I knew nothing, *nothing* about the details of my father's childhood. This was not discussed in our home. The most we ever heard about the early years was maybe a fragrant memory of longed-for food from the old country, the heavy dark bread, potatoes, noodles. During the tumult of the Russian revolution, the family was often saved from outright starvation by an older brother who was in the Red Army and would smuggle food to them. There is *a lot* about food in the memoir; long passages about food. For instance, in Cuba—a happier, more satisfying time—my father describes dinner on a farm in Santiago de Cuba, in the interior of his host country.

Let's get back to the afternoon meal. The food was plentiful. Large plates of rice with chicken, black beans, dried bananas, a bowl of meat soup with garbanzos, dessert and coffee (demi-tasse) espresso. Breakfast was café con leche (coffee with hot milk) with

*dried bananas. There wasn't any kind of bread, simply because
there were no facilities to bake bread for miles around.*

This detailed menu is recalled more than 60 years after the meal
by an old man who had experienced starvation as a child. He may have
forgotten the extreme privation, but his body and his appetite surely
remembered.

The memoir is strikingly haphazard. It took me the better part of
an afternoon to compose a rough chronology of the years before Cuba.
I had to ferret out the references to his siblings to confirm what I dimly
remembered, that there were eight siblings originally. Their names?
In the chronicle, all the boys have names, none of the girls. I had to
reconstruct the birth order of his siblings from fragments here and
there. Three of the siblings are unaccounted for. I have no idea what
happened to them or where they ended up. The lack of coherence is
meaningful. Trauma disrupts memory. Some memories (the traumatic
ones) are engraved in laser-like detail; but sequencing is patchy.

Two directly contradictory narratives of how my father came to the
U.S illustrate the most striking and almost incomprehensible instance
of disrupted memory in my father's memoir. In narrative #1 he comes
in legally through Canada during the Franklin Delano Roosevelt
administration. In narrative #2 he comes, I suppose illegally, on a boat
smuggled in by "some Arabs" during a treacherous voyage across the
Straits of Florida, and then conveyed by car North and deposited in
the Bronx with some reluctant relatives who had no idea that he was
coming. Oh, and this was before FDR became President.

A few months before re-reading this "autobiography," as my father
termed it, I attended a lecture in which audience members were asked if
they had lost close relatives in the Holocaust. I raised my hand. Then I
stared at it. I really had no reason to think I had lost relatives. My upraised
hand was obviously lying. My father's family died at the hands of Stalin in
Russia, another kind of Holocaust. That was always my understanding.
Turns out my hand knew something I didn't. Amidst the confusing
chronicle of my father's childhood, lies this startling sentence fragment:

[If it] wouldn't have been for that decision [to go to Cuba],
my sister and I would now lay in a common grave with my
Mother and my older sister Pearl and the rest of the relatives,
all liquidated by the Nazis.

Having moved back to Pinsk, my grandmother and aunt (what happened to the other children?) were in a position to be killed when the Germans invaded Poland in 1939. I never heard any mention, any reference to this tragedy so near to all of us. Never. It was not discussed or alluded to by my father, until he wrote this memoir. There it is more or less buried. Before we read the memoir, my siblings and I had no idea that our grandmother Esther and our aunt Pearl were buried in a mass grave in Poland, probably in or near Pinsk, by German or Polish Nazis. I mention their names here to provide something of a memorial, for there is otherwise none.

Ordinary children with ordinary childhoods demonstrate a kind of benign dissociation. They can play make-believe, be Snow White or a pirate and still be present when it is time to come to dinner. Trauma fixates dissociation; there is an arrest. That is what occurred with my father. The fluidity between partitioned states of mind goes rigid in the highly dissociative individual, and it does so to preserve sanity. In someone like Emma this is at its most dramatic. The part-selves have identities. The boundaries are rigid and lack flexibility. Each part is a specialist of sorts: this one goes to work and maybe even performs very well at work; that one scares off possible threats by taking on a menacing posture and demeanor, and (hopefully) doesn't show up at work. The parts do not readily communicate or even know of each other's existence.

In someone like my father, the trauma goes firmly underground, unremembered until something, like a life review toward the end of life, allows it, calls it forward. The boundaries between states are not so fixed that he doesn't have access when he turns his attention in that direction, but mostly he is decidedly *un-mindful* of these early experiences.

There are so many startling instances of fairly rigid boundaries in my father's tale: he sees a horrendous slaughter on the street and by the next day forgets about it. He watches the truck go by with the limbs of human beings hanging off the side and feels nothing. He speculates that he must have felt fear, but doesn't remember it. Not remembering that you witnessed death and assassination close up at a young age is an example of dissociation employed in the service of self-protection from overwhelming experience, the very definition of trauma.

The paradox of dissociation is that it is ideally adaptive at the time of implementation and so limiting and constraining in the long run. The more trauma there is, the more rigid are the boundaries between selves. My father's secrets were sequestered from his later self. It was only as an elderly adult, just a few years from death, that he could safely remember his own history. By committing himself to writing a memoir for his grandchildren, he put himself back in a state where he could retrieve previously sequestered memory. My father's survival during the times of privation, violence and loss depended on what he referred to as "hardened immunity:" an excellent phrase to describe the split between emotion and narrative. One of my trauma teachers spoke about memories split into three parts under the pressure of overwhelming experience: story, image and emotion. One might have the story of what happened, but no pictures or emotion. There could be flashes, pictures, without story. The dissociative deck can be shuffled in many different ways. This is strikingly obvious in my father's "autobiography."

My uncle David got lost along with the trauma of my father's childhood. As far as I can tell, this is an irretrievable loss. Large limbs of the family tree were lopped off by war, genocide, and a mystery.

Ezekiel: "The fathers ate sour grapes, and the children's teeth were set on edge."

Are my father's early experiences, unremembered, dissociated and lodged in his largely unexamined life, part of my story as a trauma therapist as well? I have never thought so before attempting this memoir. It never seemed to register with my father what I did for a living, what my professional identity was, so I had no reason to think it had anything to do with him. And I have always liked to think of myself as self-made, fashioning myself anew, separating and healing myself from a difficult family history.

Recent findings in the field of trauma research strongly indicate that trauma-induced changes can and do get passed on to the next generation. Not surprisingly, who my father became was altered by his experiences in Russia. But now it is thought that who he was *epigenetically* was changed as well, and some of those changes were passed on to the next generation, i.e. me and my siblings.

Dr. Rachel Yehuda, who studies epigenetics, explains it this way: genetics comprise the computer; a profound change in the environment, such as trauma, changes the software, the expression of those genes. This change in software is passed on to the next generation. To name only one startling finding, if your parents had PTSD, if your parents were Holocaust survivors, or survivors of war, torture and famine, or abuse survivors, you are three times more likely to respond to a traumatic circumstance—such as a car accident—with PTSD than those in a control group. This is alarming.

So my hyper-reactive stomach, my chronic back problems, my sleep disturbances may all be somehow related to this post traumatic software program. But perhaps my resilience and resourcefulness are legacy as well. My father made his way on his own when he was not quite 16 years old, travelling 6,000 miles alone, adapting to a totally new culture, learning a new language that had nothing in common with his mother tongue, not even an alphabet. And he did the latter twice!

Yehuda notes that an extraordinarily large number of people with Holocaust legacies become healers. They look to fix that which is broken. Perhaps that's part of my legacy too.

acknowledgements

As I approach the task of thanking all those who helped me to bring this book to fruition, I am able to finally understand why this section often runs to several paragraphs and often several pages. It literally takes a village to bring a memoir of treatment to a wide readership, or as wide a readership as I can muster. While writing is a lonely business, in my case it could not have become an actual, completed work without the help of several communities.

My gratitude begins and ends with Sara Taber, my writing mentor, teacher, careful reader and finally friend who had enough faith to invite me into her memoir writing class wherein I was able to conceive of and shape these pages. Roger Friedman, Desiree Magney, Alex Viets, Barbara Kazdan, Selby McPhee, Kathleen Frank, Wokie Lesher listened carefully to my drafts and helped me hone them into narratives that made sense to those not privy to the arcane language and conceptual world of trauma therapists.

Roz Beroza showed interest in my writing when I was not so interested myself and urged me to go further with it than I would have without her encouragement and lively interest. I owe her gratitude as well.

Catherine Lowry was instrumental in helping me to clarify my reactions to both my experiences with Emma and all the parts that were evoked in me by reviewing and narrating the story of our work together. I don't think I would have been able to reach as deeply into my own biography without her very astute assistance.

The peer supervision group with whom I sipped coffee weekly for over twenty years believed Emma, believed me and helped me to untangle the sometimes bewildering system of selves that Emma struggled with. Ethel Decter, Diane Roehm, Debbie Russ, Claire Ciliatta, Judith Wolfe were by my side throughout a tumultuous treatment.

Elana Benatar, Cynthia Margolies, and Sara Taber read the entire book with care and strengthened it immeasurably along the way. Each brought their special expertise to this task.

Many thanks to Carol Skolnick who did the final copy editing.

The Arnold Richards, Tamar Schwartz, and all the people at IP Books have been a pleasure to work with.

Sarah Benatar and Itzhak Benatar both provided critical technical assistance as well as emotional support on an as needed basis; both were needed frequently. My husband Itzhak put up with a lot obsessive thinking as I struggled with the manuscript and encouraged me when my motivation flagged.

It is of course to Emma that I owe that greatest debt of gratitude, both for what I learned from her and for her brave and generous permission to tell our story.

www.ingramcontent.com/pod-product-compliance
Lightning Source LLC
Chambersburg PA
CBHW050731030426
42336CB00012B/1510